# KNOWING WOMAN

# KNOWING WOMAN

*A Feminine Psychology*

by

Irene Claremont de Castillejo

Published by
G. P. PUTNAM'S SONS
New York
for the C. G. Jung Foundation for Analytical Psychology

# ACKNOWLEDGEMENTS

*Some of the sections of this book have been published in pamphlet form by The Guild of Pastoral Psychology, and others have appeared in* Harvest, *the annual publication of the Jungian Analytical Psychology Club, London, with whose kind permission they are reprinted here.*

*Robert Frost's poem 'Escapist - Never' is quoted from* The Poetry of Robert Frost *edited by Edward Connery Lathem by permission of Jonathan Cape Ltd and Holt, Rinehart and Winston, Inc. Copyright © 1962 by Robert Frost. Copyright © 1969 by Holt, Rinehart and Winston, Inc. The extract from Christopher Fry's play* The Dark is Light Enough *is quoted by permission of the Oxford University Press.*

# PREFACE

I describe here what I have learned of woman's present psychology. Perhaps I am only describing myself. But in twenty years as a Jungian analyst I have been concerned by the break-up of marriages, by misunderstandings between man and man, and between men and women. I have tried to follow the psychology of different kinds of women and their effects on men, and I have wondered about our personal as well as our collective responsibility for the state of society around us.

Women are today face to face with some unforeseen consequences of their new equality with men.

*May 1967*                                                                 I. C. de C.

# CONTENTS

# I

# *Meeting*

THE OTHER DAY a friend asked me a question which set me thinking. 'Is it exhausting to listen and talk to people all day?' I answered as anyone else might have done. 'Sometimes very exhausting, sometimes not at all.'

Then I began to wonder on what this question of fatigue depended. Certainly not on the amount I personally put out. It almost seemed at first sight as though it were an inverse ratio. One is often less tired when one contributes a lot to a conversation than if one is a passive listener.

As I considered actual conversations with other persons, not only those in working hours, I began to realize that the question was not one of fatigue or lack of fatigue, but rather of fatigue or refreshment.

And suddenly it was so clear and obvious that I could not imagine why I had not seen it before. We are only exhausted when talking to other people if we do not meet them, when one or both of us are hiding behind screens.

On the rare occasions when we are fortunate enough to meet someone, there is no question of fatigue. Both are refreshed, for something has happened. It is as though a door had opened, and life suddenly takes on new meaning.

Why is it then that we meet so seldom? The curious thing is that we spend our lives not meeting people. All day we mix with others, in the bus, in shops, at work or play; but it may be that not once in the course of days or weeks or months do we meet any one of these people in such a way that a vibration is set up between the two. Nothing happens.

After the business of the day we go home and join our families, where it is quite easy for the various members to rub alongside one another without meeting each other at all, and without anybody noticing the fact.

Meetings are of course on various levels. There are meetings of the body and meetings of the mind; meetings in realms of the intellect and during the companionship of daily living or working together. Meetings can be of every conceivable degree of closeness or duration, on one level only or on all at once. There can be meetings of mystical spiritual intensity. But on no level does mere physical proximity or mutual exchange of ideas necessarily constitute a meeting. Frequently husbands and wives have the closest physical intimacy for years and yet have no real meeting. Each is wrapped away in an isolation of his own.

For there to be a meeting, it seems as though a third, a something else, is always present. You may call it Love, or the Holy Spirit. Jungians would say that it is the presence of the Self. If this 'Other' is present, there cannot have failed to be a meeting.

Duration has nothing to do with it. Nor have common interests. The touch of a hand may suffice. I can recall some conversations with total strangers which have never lost their flavour because in some inexplicable way there had for a little while been a real meeting.

I have never forgotten the smile of a bus conductor as I alighted from a bus at the age of twenty. It was a smile shared. We never saw one another again, nor needed to, but for a few seconds we really met. I have written a little poem about it:

> A million footprints
> On solitary sand
>     Are washed away,
> Yet the fragrance of a smile
> Between a bus conductor
> And a girl alighting
> Has lingered in the air
> Full forty years.

Even in as brief a meeting as that, some infinitesimal but indestructible thing has been added to the whole atmosphere.

This something which springs into being at every real meeting is not identical with sympathy. Sympathy can be resented, it can even be harmful, tearing down the banner of courage held high. But a meeting can never harm. It adds another banner to that already flying.

This something which springs into being is more than thoughts shared. (It can be devastating to be asked what one is thinking.) Sharing is on a different level altogether. It brings people together and helps them to grow in the same direction. Some sharing is required for any lasting relationship; but sharing is not in itself what I am talking about, nor is relationship. I am talking of the capacity to meet and to be met. Such meetings, from time to time, are the essential growing points in any live relationship, but they may also happen where the term relationship could hardly be used.

It is possible, I am sure, for more than two people to meet at the same time. The happening of a presence may occur between three, or perhaps even four. 'When two or three are gathered together in My Name, there shall I be.' This is probably the same Presence, as in meetings between two, of which I have already spoken.

The modern emphasis on relationships between only two people can sometimes degenerate into mere exclusiveness and a self-conscious sharing which, valuable though it is, may become an infringement of privacy, or an abuse of intimacy. Deliberate sharing is sometimes as dangerous as sympathy. New ideas which are forming in the depths of the mind can actually be destroyed or crippled by being shared too soon. It is like dragging a baby from the womb before it is ready to be born, or digging up a bulb to watch the sprouting of the roots. Respect for another person's privacy is as important as sharing thoughts. The deepest communication will in any case take place in moments of silence.

Sometimes I wonder if it is wise to work directly at relationship. What matters is to be centred oneself, willing and ready, always ready for the moments or hours of meeting when they come. Then the relationship can be trusted to take care of itself.

Every time, I think, it is one's own attitude, not the relationship, on which one needs to work. It is a fact that in any partnership, if one of the partners becomes quite clear *in himself* what it is that the situation requires, the chances are it will not even be necessary to voice it; the other will somehow pick up the point and comply, with no words said. Internal clarity anywhere seems to have the effect of an invisible guiding force which can be trusted to affect not only personal relationships, but outer situations. For the person who has achieved inner clarity, new paths appear and doors open without the need to knock.

I think unwillingness to be met is the element which is so often left out in our thinking. Women in particular, who know that relationship is primarily their concern, try to bring everything out into the open. But if a man is unwilling to be met he feels a

victim. So does a woman when she is urged to express what she
cannot formulate, even if she would. Such attempts at forcible
sharing effect no magic.

In the analytical hour one has an unusual opportunity of noticing this phenomenon of meeting. Analyst and patient do not
always meet. If the analyst is exhausted after an hour he may be
quite sure that he has failed to meet his patient. He may have been
too active, pouring himself out when it was not required. He may
have been too passive, feeling the vitality sucked out of him
against his will. In neither case will there have been that dynamic
meeting which engenders healing.

Willingness to be met on the part of the analyst, no less than on
that of the patient, is essential. Sometimes the analyst is unwilling
to dive deep enough to meet the submerged patient, the refusal
being a sound instinct for self-preservation. Sometimes he may be
unduly afraid to follow into the obscure and diverse paths to
which a patient beckons him. But in either case there is no meeting, and no healing. It is only the moments of true meeting which
open the door to an illumination that heals, and refreshes both
patient and analyst alike.

Exactly the same kind of situation exists in daily life. How is it
then that we fail to meet so often?

There seem to be three main reasons. The first is that we are
often living on a different level of awareness from the other
person. The second is that one of us at least is often playing a
role, or is somehow possessed. And the third is that we fail to
listen to each other. I will deal with these three barriers in this
order.

I think it helps us to understand the problem of meeting if we
realize that all the time, whether we are men or women, we are
living on several distinct levels of awareness. In particular there is
a very clear difference between the focused consciousness of mankind, and a diffuse awareness which has not been fully appreci-
ated.

Focused consciousness has emerged over thousands of years
from the unconscious, and is still emerging. All our education is an
attempt to produce and sharpen it in order to give us power to
look at things and analyse them into their component parts, in
order to give us the ability to formulate ideas, and the capacity to
change, invent, create. It is this focused consciousness which we

are all using in the everyday world all the time. Without it there would have been no culture and no scientific discoveries.

It is however not the only kind of consciousness. Most children are born with and many women retain, a diffuse awareness of the wholeness of nature, where everything is linked with everything else and they feel themselves to be part of an individual whole. It is from this layer of the psyche which is not yet broken into parts that come the wise utterances of children. Here lies the wisdom of artists, and the words and parables of prophets, spoken obliquely so that only those who have ears to hear can hear and the less mature will not be shattered.

If we realize that on the whole the basic masculine attitude to life is that of focus, division and change; and the feminine (in either sex) is more nearly an attitude of acceptance, an awareness of the unity of all life and a readiness for relationship, then we can accept a rough division of the psyche into masculine and feminine. But today, when masculine and feminine characteristics are so interwoven in people of both sexes, it may be clearer to speak of 'focused consciousness' on the one hand and 'diffuse awareness' on the other, knowing that these qualities belong to both men and women in varying degrees.

It is important to remember, however, that diffuse awareness more commonly pertains to women. From early life the small girl tends to delight in everything that concerns life and living while the small boy shows passionate interest in what makes the wheels go round, or why the kettle steams when it boils. Wheels and possible uses of steam usually leave little girls cold. Similarly most women feel akin to trees and running water, and have a sense of belonging under a night sky, and all of them are linked with the rhythm of the moon. It is men who want to go there and explore its extinct volcanoes. However, the man in love will have been temporarily inspired by the realm of diffuse awareness and may perhaps voice it later in a poem. The woman who looks through the telescope will for the time being have her mind clearly focused and may even write a scientific treatise.

Unfortunately, while we are standing on one level, the other seems such nonsense that we tend to repudiate it wholly. It is a real dilemma. I offend my head or I offend my heart. And always it is one's heart which finds itself in the greater dilemma, as this is the sphere which ordinarily has no voice. This problem of different levels is not confined to communication between different people.

There is a constant lack of harmony within the mind of the same person. How often one argues with oneself, because the two inner voices cannot meet. What, for instance, should I do when a beggar comes to my door? 'Give help,' says one voice. 'Don't be a fool,' says the other. 'I can't possibly slam the door in his face,' says the first voice. 'You are only encouraging vagrancy,' says the second. The two truths do not coincide. They often do not even impinge on one another.

Those who are able to stand firmly on the basis of rational common sense will shut the door in the beggar's face, more or less politely, convinced that the slight, just discernible twinges of guilt at their own lack of charity are signs of childish sentiment which they should have outgrown long ago. This is the attitude of our masculine culture, the fruit of our focused consciousness: a fruit we have won at the cost of hardening our hearts. But for those who are aware that all life is one, and that what is done to any is done to all, it is inconceivable to refuse the beggar.

This diffuse level is where children live, until we educate them out of it, educate them to be more sensible. However, any adult who lives solely on this diffuse level comes near to being like the Idiot in Dostoievsky's novel. The Idiot returning, as a young man, to normal society after years of insanity, sees life with the simplicity of a child, and in every situation reacts with a direct and frank naïveté which shows up the edifice that society has built in its stark hypocrisy. Dostoievsky's Idiot faithfully portrays the feminine sphere of acceptance without any masculine discrimination whatsoever. With the innocence of a child he knows no boundaries for love and sees no sense in hiding truth. He leaps over wire fences, heedless of their warning barbs. His willingness to meet and to be met is unconditional. The havoc he causes brings his world crashing about his ears, and his only hope is to take refuge in insanity once more.

Focused consciousness and diffuse awareness are not only impotent to convince one another, they can even become mutually destructive. Over awareness of diffuse feminine values may paralyse us and make action impossible in the outer world. On the other hand a too focused consciousness may render the wisdom from the feminine layer of our psyche invisible, and burn it up with too bright a flame. As I write, a beautiful many-coloured butterfly has alighted upon my reading lamp, fallen and died. This is what happens to diffuse awareness.

Unfortunately education does not help us. The sensitive boy, aware of things beneath the surface, finds from the moment he goes to school, that his innate wisdom is not honoured. He will hide it away first from his fellows to avoid their scoffing, and finally from himself.

The girl, often taught by women who have more interest in ideas than experience of living, has hard work to keep hold of her innate femininity. Success at school depends on devoting her time and energy to masculine pursuits; a good job may demand a university degree. It is a path which she gladly treads because it has been denied her so long. But the feminine layer of diffuse awareness can very easily be submerged, and if it is lost, the ability to meet and allow herself to be met in later life is rendered much more difficult.

How can a woman live out her masculine side and at the same time be her own feminine self?

I know one young married woman who was sufficiently alive to this problem to detect that the irritation between herself and her husband, after her long day's work in an office, was not due to fatigue alone. She arranged to get home from work a good hour before her husband so that she had a breathing space in which to throw off her masculine side, and collect her more feminine self before he came in. When it was not possible to get home early she asked her husband to delay his own return. He then spent the hour in a pub reading the paper. I am not advocating this as a solution, but the effect of this odd arrangement was miraculous. Irritable evenings vanished.

The whole question of being there to be met, of being really present, is extraordinarily subtle. The trouble begins when two people are trying to communicate, unaware that they are speaking from different levels. They may, for instance, be discussing the use of nuclear weapons. The one who is on the level of focused consciousness will argue quite rationally about the possibility of agreement between Russia and the West, and the futility of consenting to the suspension of tests or disarmament without control. While the one who is at that moment on the level of diffuse awareness will be in despair. 'Can't you see the criminal stupidity of the whole thing? Who cares whether Russia or China may play us false? The lives of posterity are at stake — we should refuse to have anything to do with nuclear arms here and now, whatever anyone else does. Can't you see?'

No, he can't. He will begin arguing about the possibility of making 'clean bombs', and may add that: 'In any case the percentage of children affected in the future is so infinitesimally small when you compare it with the population of the world. The important thing is to preserve the freedom of the individual and this is why we can take no risks.'

And by this time the other party is mentally, or actually, wringing her hands with frustration and wanting to scream. (I have assumed for the moment she was a woman, though it is often the other way round.) These two can go on arguing forever, but neither will have the slightest effect on the other because they are speaking from different levels which, like parallel lines, never meet.

I had a clear example the other day of meeting, and failing to meet, the same girl in the space of half an hour. I knew her well. She came to see me and talked at length about her mother. I got more and more bored until I became convinced that this was not what she had come to say. So I asked her, 'What did you really come to tell me?' She was very annoyed and said this was exactly what she had come about and it wasn't her fault if I was bored, which I obviously was. I apologized. Then she said she was all muddled now and didn't know any longer what she had come for. I apologized some more for having confused her. Finally, she burst into tears and began to tell me all the things she had already told me about her mother. But this time we met because it was *she* who was talking. The things she said were the same things that I had already heard, but a different person was speaking.

It transpired that while travelling to me in the underground a poem had been forming in her mind. She was no doubt on the level of diffuse awareness and was groping for formulation. When she arrived at my door she was still on this level with her poem. But it was in fact her mother she had come to talk about, so she had handed the matter over to her masculine spokesman, the animus, who lives on the level of focused consciousness, and instructed him to carry on. He did so, telling me all the things she wanted me to know, but just because it was not herself speaking, I could not meet her, I could not even listen.

The interesting thing is that in order to meet this girl I did not have to go to the level of the poem. She was not wanting to talk about the poem. It was she who came to the level of focused consciousness and met me there, but this time co-operating with her masculine spokesman on that level instead of just handing over to him and absenting herself as she had at the beginning. Please note that she and I had to be on the same level before it was possible for us to meet at all.


Now this uncertainty as to where we stand brings me to my second topic, the barrier of not being truly *present* in order to be met. One of the main reasons why we so often fail to meet other people is that we are so seldom really there.

To begin with we are so often identified with our roles in society, and no one can meet a role. I cannot meet a doctor, a civil servant, a hospital nurse, or a shop girl unless these throw off their disguise and look me in the eye – any more than I can meet an acted Hamlet, though I might conceivably meet a real one. Similarly to be met I must be myself.

This facile but mistaken belief that we are identical with the role we act is common to everybody. But the fact that we are not always ourselves is recognized in common speech. 'So and so is not himself today' we say, or 'Tom was beside himself' (an odd place to be). Or 'He was like one possessed' we say. Possession by some part of the psyche for which we do not take full responsibility is a more common situation then we like to realize — though we often notice it in others. Sometimes we can actually hear ourselves saying things which we know we do not mean, or things we had made up our minds not to mention; and we are sometimes horrified at the knowledge that it is our tongue and lips which are being used. It is as though we were listening to another person speaking.

Most women have had this sort of shattering experience, all the more disturbing because both the hearer and she herself are left shaken and wondering if these strange words spoken might not be the truth. They sometimes are; an idea uttered has been given tangible life and can never be unspoken, no matter how often it is denied.

So we are brought straight up against the question: Who am I? What is this mysterious thing that calls itself 'I'? It is of course the 'I' which says yes or no, it is the 'I' which chooses. And one of the choices before us at any time is on which level, the focused or the diffuse, I take my stand.

Mixing of the levels inadvertently can cause diabolical confusion and one sees it occurring every day. For example, the wife who asks her husband which is more important to him, she or his work, is standing on her feminine truth of relationship where love is what matters. If the husband has a glimmering of understanding he will meet her on her level and reply, 'Why you, of course.' But when she follows this up with a plea that, in that case, he should put her first and give his work less time and energy — she has jumped without noticing it on to the plane of everyday where man's work needs first place. He feels he has been tricked, as indeed he has unintentionally, by an innocent confusion of levels.

The worst kind of confusion, absence, or hiding behind a screen, occurs when a woman unconsciously hands over to the spokesman of the level of masculine focused consciousness which Jung named the animus and — as in the case I have shown — remains hidden herself in the background. She then allows him to pronounce all sorts of collective opinions which are not quite relevant to the situation, and are not what she herself thinks or feels.

This is called 'animus possession' and I shall deal with this phenomenon in another chapter. We can almost always detect his presence by his irrelevance. However, it is not the fault of the animus if what he says is beside the point. Whenever a woman hears this sort of thing inside her own head, she should call for help. The voice is always false.

Tears, spontaneous, genuine tears will, without fail, dispel any form of animus possession. (It was when the girl wept that I was able to meet her.) Tears in a woman should be welcomed, not repressed. They wash away all falsity, and leave her naked, truly herself, and ready to be met.

A man can also be possessed when, unbeknown to himself, the unconscious feminine — or anima — has taken over (a state of possession expressed more by moods than words, as the feminine is seldom vocal). The moods may range from caprice to irresponsibility, from sulks to vanity, from sentimentality to sheer bad temper. He has stumbled inadvertently into the sphere which he does not at all understand, and wonders why he is so ill at ease.

On the other hand, a man who knowingly enters the feminine level of diffuse awareness will be able to use his natural gift for formulation to express the wisdom that he finds there.

In this kind of achievement artists are supremely important. A creative artist is a person who, in spite of the pressure of education and the need to adapt to a society based on focused consciousness, succeeds in never losing his contact with the field of diffuse awareness where the unbroken connection of all growing things still reigns. This explains the artist's state of continual conflict, and his often strange behaviour. His art is not the result of a one-sided development, as has often been suggested, but of a greater capacity to live the whole of his personality; and whether his art sees the light of day or not, he has done something of immense significance, not only for himself but for society as a whole.[1]

It is not only our uncertainty as to who we are or where we are standing which makes us hide behind a screen; it is also our fear of being led along dangerous paths if we embark upon the business of meeting someone else: the fear of being taken advantage of, and the terror of possible involvement which we had never intended. But usually a clear knowledge of where we stand, and the ability to change our stance, allays these fears.

The problem of the beggar is a case in point. A beggar came to my door one day. He had only one arm and a heavy basket. I was in a feminine mood. I did not want his goods, but he put the basket down, looked me in the eyes and said, 'I am so tired, could you give me a cup of tea?' Across the kitchen table while I fed him, the beggar and I talked and really met. As he was about to leave he shook me by the hand, tried to draw me to him for a kiss and whispered, 'When is your husband out?' I did not allow the kiss, but I retained his hand for I did not want to hurt him. I shook my head and answered, 'You must not come again. Next time I shall not be here.' He never came again. He was not meaning to take advantage. He was merely caught on the level of diffuse awareness where we had both met.

It was of course my ability to change from that level to one of common sense which had enabled me to talk to him so freely.

Meeting is of course always something of a miracle, and cannot be planned nor explained. Mercifully, real, vibrant meetings which always entail the presence of the mysterious 'third', are vouchsafed us from time to time whether we are conscious or not.

---

[1] I owe this observation about artists to Neumann, who first defined the difference between focused and diffuse awareness. Neumann says that this fact applies to the creative artist in men, as that of women is more complicated.

They befall us as a grace, and stand out like beacons, and no forceful removal of barriers will, of its own accord, bring them about. But I should like to conclude this chapter by discussing what I have called the third great barrier to true, genuine meeting.

This barrier is the failure of communication: that we very often do not say what we really mean, and those who are at the receiving end equally often fail to listen.

Communication often fails to take place because we do not know ourselves well enough to be clear what we want to say. This is particularly true of many social groups. The worker, for example, who demands higher wages may not have recognized that boredom in our technological age is a more fundamental cause of his unrest than his pay cheque. But he will talk about his pay cheque, and the real cause will remain unmentioned.

Even highly conscious groups such as doctors are not necessarily conscious enough to voice their real complaint. G.P.s for instance, have been vociferous about their unjust remuneration and inferior status in the medical hierarchy, but I have never heard them mention what is much more likely to be the fundamental nature of their unhappiness: that the *archetype of healer* which has sustained and nourished them throughout the centuries has fallen from their shoulders leaving them as little cogs in the great machine of modern medical practice. It is not a greater share of the world's wealth they lack, but 'mana'.

The dwindling congregations in our churches is another example. Men have not ceased to be spiritually hungry, but the people to whom the priest, or minister, or rabbi addresses his words have changed, and no longer understand his language.

However, I do not propose to deal with any particular problem of communication here. I wish to deal with a much more curious failing: the difficulty of listening.

I remember when I was at school, attending a small class of advanced mathematics for the sixth form, where the teacher one day carefully explained some new theory. Did we all understand? I admitted I did not. The teacher explained again. Was it clear now? I shook my head. 'I am sorry, I still don't quite see.' Once more with infinite patience the teacher went through the whole thing. Again I shook my head. Then suddenly the light dawned. 'The truth is,' I said brightly, with delight at the discovery, 'I haven't been listening.' That is the point, we do not listen.

Miss Whetnall has written a very interesting book on deaf children and has pointed out that deafness in children, with resulting dumbness, is by no means always due to a faulty hearing mechanism. It may be due to the failure on the part of the child in the interpretation of the meaning of a sound. Sometimes, she tells us, the parents of a child who appears to be deaf stop talking to it so that it gets no practice in attaching meaning to a sound. Miss Whetnall has discovered that patiently talking to the child individually, not teaching him to lip read, but talking to him audibly, can sometimes rectify this. The child begins to apprehend and will spontaneously begin to talk. The value of residual hearing has apparently been overlooked hitherto in teaching so called deaf and dumb children to speak.

Miss Whetnall has also realized that correct testing of deafness in a child depends not only on the loudness of a sound, but on its relevance. A deaf child may not flicker an eyelid at a loud bang behind him, for it is only one more meaningless sound, yet it may turn round to investigate if a teaspoon is tinkled in a cup.

This book on deaf children seems to throw light on the whole problem of listening in adult life. It seems that we can only give attention to a topic when we can give meaning to it — otherwise we turn away or think of something else.

Certainly, as we mature, we make more and more conscious choices of the fields of ideas we will cultivate. And it may be that man is helped to specialize by an actual increase in deafness or 'screening out' fields other than his own – as though the openness of the child to *all* impressions has to give way to canalization for some and deafness towards others. He has, as it were, to produce a sieve which will let through only relevant sounds.

The growing deafness, or rather inability to listen, of the adult in the course of specialization, certainly meets us at every turn. People who are materially oriented are unable often to hear words that were meaningful to them as children. As an extreme example, many children seem capable of hearing overtones in the word God which will be wholly repudiated by them at a later age. So much so that if anyone talks to them as adults about God they cease to listen. Others continue to hear overtones of increasing richness in the word God. Communication between these two groups then becomes impossible.

There is an inner listening as well as an outer which can be learned or ignored. When only one of these hearing skills is acquired it becomes well nigh impossible for the exponents of either the inner or outer process to communicate their experience to the other.

Mercifully most of us have experience of both worlds. But we do not always know which we are standing in at any particular time and this is one reason why communication often breaks down. The frustration caused by vain attempts to communicate between inner and outer often arouses anger and contempt on both sides.

However, this impatience of one with the other, which precludes either from attempting to listen to what the other is saying is largely a defence reaction. For in point of fact each attitude does dangerously menace the other. We do not generally recognize the extent to which, nor how easily, we can undermine the whole groundwork upon which another individual has built his life. Often a woman will provoke emotion and leave her man floundering in it while she goes off singing. She does this when she can't stand his cool reasonableness any longer, but although emotion clears the air for her, to the man it can be disruptive, prevent him from thinking, and make work impossible. Conversely the very clarity of a man's thought can be destructive. A valuable idea which is pushing its way up through the dark in a woman's mind, may be utterly withered and destroyed if an arc lamp of focused consciousness is thrown upon it. A woman who is simply trying to hold on to her diffuse awareness may feel as though she is being punched in the solar plexus by a battering ram if a man hurls a mass of logic at her.

In either case the very foundations of our whole attitude to life are threatened. So we shut our ears to one another, and vociferously try to shout the other down.

In the same way, in international matters, the East and the West often do not listen to one another because they have already decided that their opponent cannot be trusted. And even in government, where one would hope for a reasonable exchange of views prior to legislation, discussion often degenerates into a clever scoring of points, and listening plays little part.

In less extreme cases the exposition of another point of view may even be felt as menacing when there is nothing intrinsically wrong with it. It is the disturbance of emotion and thought which terrifies us and makes us put up our defence of not listening to whatever produces this alarmingly uncomfortable state. We all recognize this feeling, which can vary in degree from merely getting hot under the collar to positive panic, whenever the validity of our own attitude towards life seems threatened. Yet the first step towards any synthesis of the two half truths known and expressed by our opposing kinds of consciousness, lies in their learning to *listen* to one another.

Of course the technique of listening is different for each group. The exponents of diffuse awareness have to learn to focus. This is their weakest point, as their insight has always been dependent on a vision which is blurred just because it is so wide. On the other hand the people who have always trusted their ability to draw logical deductions from proven facts, need to listen by reading between the lines, as it were. It is no use their taking the words at their face value and then proving they make no sense.

Even in actual reading this is so. One can examine a book sentence by sentence to discover what each sentence actually means. Or one can blur one's focus and read the work as a whole without analysis. This is a reading between the lines. The effect of this method is completely different. One may find it difficult or impossible to make a precis afterwards of what the author has said, but one often receives a staggering impact which, paradoxically, can never be forgotten. I remember reading Maurice Nicoll's *Living Time* in this way. The book made a lasting impression on me though I have never been able to tell anyone else what the book was about.

Unfortunately, although the spoken or written word is our greatest tool of communication it is deceptively blunt. Even an unemotional word like 'society' means one thing to the labour leader, another to the social worker, and something even more different to the debutante. Still more troublesome are words which have emotional overtones, like love or God. These convey meanings which are worlds apart to different people. The old man with a white beard in the sky would hardly recognize himself in the abstract guise in which he is clothed today. Similarly the word love can be stretched from a simple sex encounter to the most sublime mystical union. When using these words we may be approximately near one another's meaning, but in my analytical work I am constantly reminded how very approximate it is, and that the use of words can build a wall between people as easily as it opens a road of communication.

In effect we have to live a paradox. To close our ears to the irrelevant is a cultural necessity for the preservation of our own individualities. When we have found our true individual road we have to keep to it. To follow every bypath in outer life gets us nowhere. To follow the call of every voice in the inner world leads to disorientation.

This ability to select is one of man's greatest gifts. But the ability to meet other men is another great quality, and this involves opening those ears which we have been so busily closing in order to select.

As we begin to achieve this we start to lower one of the great barriers to meeting.

# II

# Responsibility and Shadow

TODAY THE WORLD'S problems are too technical and too vast for ordinary individuals to feel they have the power to influence them. Our educational institutions still pay lip service to the importance of training our children to think and take responsibility. But once outside school or college we plunge them into a society where independent thought ceases to be an asset. The government employee (and more and more of us are working for the government) knows that he can never take final responsibility. The last word rests with the bureaucracy.

So most of us shrug our shoulders, turn our backs on the monstrous problems of our civilization, and enjoy life as best we can. Our sense of responsibility for the outer world has left us.

Curiously enough there are two forces at work aggravating this situation. The first is the obsession for conformity which has overtaken us. We buy the same things, see the same television programmes, read the same newspapers, and more and more of us go to the same type of schools. We conform to the opinion of our set, a union, a church, a business company, an undefined company of so-called free thinkers, or a particular psychological school.

The second force at work is, curiously enough, modern psychology itself, which is making the great mistake of urging people to turn inwards, and deal with their problems inside themselves, rather than dealing with them in external life. Psychologists are so often taught to regard their sole contribution to society as lying within the sphere of self-knowledge, that they tend to evade the outer aspect of a man's responsibility towards the world at large. Psychological theory claims that we tend to project our own bad qualities on the outside world, and if we withdraw our projections and deal with them inside ourselves all will be well. However, I have grave misgivings that the psychologists' insistence on this need to withdraw projections may be having the wrong results. A readiness to protest externally is an essential part of a living democracy. If we fail to voice our feelings of pleasure or horror we deprive our leaders of one of the essential factors on which their judgment rests. The psychologists' method of making individuals deal with the shadow solely *within* themselves, is making many intelligent citizens turn their backs on the problems of the outside world.

Discouragement of natural rebels is no service to a democracy. But psychologists are so scared of allowing anyone to foster anything resembling a saviour complex, that the dynamism which goes with a reforming zeal is being damped down and lost to the world. Great deeds can only be achieved when we are more than our little selves. When we are lent wings we should not reject them.

Today the normal appears to be the modern goal. The normal? Could anything be more uninspiring? If a man can be got back into the labour market, able to carry out some dull little job, be some insignificant cog in the great anonymous machine of industry or Civil Service, the psychiatrist considers he has ably done his job; though he plunges the man back into the very society and the very work which had made him ill.

We tend too much to level down. Christ would have fared badly had he lived today. He might so easily, in his agony, have found his way to a mental hospital and been rendered fit to keep a normal job. The Romans did better when they crucified his body. They did not diminish, they enhanced his spiritual power.

Pscyhologists have inadvertently side-slipped into this dreary passion for normality. But I am not so sure that to be balanced is necessarily a virtue. Some urgent inner problem or some imbalance may actually provide the impetus for dealing with outer wrongs. The rebel who is stirred to action by injustice or cruelty to others may well have himself suffered from an inner tyrant which bullies him.

Most geniuses in whatever field are, to ordinary eyes, more than a little mad. The heavy price some artists have to pay for their unusual insight may be lack of balance. The world would have been a poorer place without Van Gogh.

The trouble is that psychologists believe they can see and explain the patterns of behaviour. On certain levels maybe they can, but let us never forget the unique unknowableness of every individual soul. Psychological thinking has seeped through into ordi-

nary life, and it is so easy to explain a situation by some
psychological slogan — yet the inner meaning may lie in a very
different place.

Parents, too, tend to see the defects and to believe they know the
complexes of their children; but if they are wise they will remember that they do *not* know the innermost truth of their children's
souls. We do *not* know the destiny to which another has been
born. We do not know where he is to rebel, which mistakes he is
to make. Perhaps some idiosyncracy or some failure to fit into
society may be that child's particular contribution to the world,
which should not be cured but fostered.

We may see the mistakes of the young but if we are wise we
must also learn to be blind; to know and yet *not* to know is one of
the paradoxical secrets of relationships.

Some course of action which seems so clearly to be leading to
disaster may contain a twist of fate which lifts it to success. That
accident whose cause was so apparent may have had an inner
meaning we cannot see. That sudden death which we think
could have been so easily avoided with greater consciousness
may not have been the tragedy it appears. The man who died
may have been needed elsewhere. We simply do not know.
Scientists discover and theologians affirm; but faced with the
mystery of life and death we know almost nothing. We can
learn from the experts, but our experience may not fit their
theories and it is our experience and our experience alone that
we should trust.

I have criticized the trend of modern psychology towards conformity, but on a deeper level it is paradoxically psychology which
is trying to help people move away from conformity by teaching
them to take internal and individual responsibility for their own
shadow.

The shadow is that part of the psyche which could and should
become conscious, yet of which we are unaware. It consists of
those characteristics we do not recognize in ourselves. Unfortunately people tend to believe that 'the shadow' means our
bad qualities. But the shadow can be bright and good as well as
dark and bad. A real virtue is often hidden away in the unconscious. For instance, a timid and shy person may show courage in
an emergency which surprises himself as much as his friends. Or
an habitually mean man may have fits of unexpected generosity

which he finds a positive embarrassment. The generosity and
courage could both be styled 'shadow qualities' because they are
unknown to their owner, but the shadow here would be bright. It
is the habitual unconsciousness of a quality that makes it a
shadow, not its badness.

Whether our shadow qualities are bad or good, we need to
know their presence, in order that we can begin to take responsibility for their effect on others and on ourselves.

Having made this clear, I am now going to talk principally about
the dark shadow qualities, as they are the most actively dangerous.

It is common knowledge that we project qualities upon other
people and dislike, or positively hate, the other person for some
characteristic which we unconsciously share ourselves. So long as
we only see black shadows on someone else, we can take no responsibility for them in ourselves. We merely hate the other
fellow.

A good way of learning to detect one's shadow is to notice what
qualities in others make us angry or irritated. We should allow
ourselves to feel irritated or angry with other people to the full.
And then when we have calmed down, if we turn our thoughts
inward and enquire whether we have some similar quality in
our own nature, on some level or another, we can generally
find it. If we can succeed in doing so, the projections we had
made on the other person will be automatically withdrawn
because it is only qualities of which we are *un*conscious that we
project.

The removal of our projections may actually make other
people nicer. Our effect on others is far greater than we suppose,
and it is difficult not to be as disagreeable as is expected of one.
This is what 'carrying a projection' means. But even if the other
person remains unpleasant — in fact he may *be* unpleasant — the
removal of our projection will enable us to see him as he is, without the anger or irritation we felt before.

The bright shadow qualities, on the other hand, of which we
are unaware, we envy in other people. I doubt if we ever envy
qualities which do not intrinsically belong to us.

An integrated individual is one who carries his own dark
shadow of undesirable qualities, frees those around him from his
projections, and by so doing actually transforms a fraction of the
evil in the world. When he carries his own bright shadow he takes

up his courage, his strength, and his dignity, and his own imaginative insight, and refuses to be bowed down by burdens which others are unknowingly projecting on to him.

Now the three shadows which we should perhaps take special note of today are the national shadow, our own personal shadow, and, darkest of all, woman's shadow.

Unconscious projection — and projection is always unconscious — is probably at the root of most wars. We project our national shadow on to other countries. Let us look first at this, since it concerns us all.

Today we spend a lot of energy rabidly hating the Russians or the Chinese for their disregard of individual life and individual liberty. We are so busy inveighing against these things in Russia and China that we do not even notice what has happened here.

On the rare occasions when I get caught in the rush hour, I see a swarm of sad tired people, with unsatisfied faces, all pushing one another for the right to stand up for an hour, jammed tightly together in a fetid atmosphere. And when I recall that these people are obliged to do this twice daily, and during the intervening hours most of them work, or evade working, at something which interests them little and often bores them excruciatingly, I wonder where is the respect for individual life of which we boast? Where is our vaunted freedom? Our thoughts are dictated by a narrow daily Press, our values are decided by advertisements and television. Our activities are curtailed by regulations and orders without number, and even our representatives in the government no longer speak from the depth of their consciences, but obey the command of the party machines.

We see these tyrannies in Russia or China and hate them with all our souls, but because we have not noticed that we are no longer free ourselves, we vent our hatred on the Chinese or Russians, instead of on the tyranny.

If only we would realize that it is here in our own country that capacity and brains and willingness to work are no longer usable unless first wrapped in a parcel of paper qualifications. It is here, in this country, that the law meddles with the private morality of individuals. It is true we can still say what we like in public, but already the tapping of private telephones is the thin end of a very ugly wedge.

This is part of our national shadow, and if we can see our

own serious defects at home we shall be able to recognize that despotism, the inevitable shadow of over-rational planning, is not a speciality of the Chinese, it is the same virus the world over.

To see this tyrannical shadow only outside in other countries leads straight to war, but to know and deal with despotism at home is to take responsibility for our share of this monster. It does not exonerate us from protesting at barbarism elsewhere, but it does give us the possibility of fighting the evil on our own ground, instead of forever thinking it is someone else's business.

So much for our national shadow. Now let us look at our personal shadow.

To take full responsibility for our own personal shadow involves having some knowledge of our inferior function, about which there seems to be some confusion in people's minds.

Let me explain this matter in psychological terms. Jung has described four ways of mental functioning: *Thinking, Feeling, Sensation,* and *Intuition. Thinking* and *feeling* he calls rational, in that when either of them are being used we are making judgments. *Thinking* analyses, *feeling* is the function which evaluates worth, whether a thing is good or bad.

The other two functions, *sensation* and *intuition* do not judge in any way; they are ways of perceiving. With our sensation we perceive how things are, whether within or without; with our intuition we have hunches of how they might be, or we perceive inner meaning and significance.

This is of course a gross over-simplification, and only intended as a reminder. In actual fact there are innumerable complexities, varieties and combinations.

A person of high intelligence will never be characterized by only one function. It is well known, however, that we tend to use one function more than the others, though we can gradually develop the use of the others also.

It is the function which is least well developed in any particular person which is called the inferior function. It could as well be called the fourth function and perhaps with less confusion.

Even those of us who are fairly all round people tend to have a fourth function which is decidedly elusive. We all know the thinkers whose feeling is so bad that they can unwittingly trample underfoot by their logic what to someone else is precious. We

know the women who are so sure of their feeling judgment that
they will tell one that something is 'so right' or 'so wrong' without
seeing the slightest need for logical proof. We know the sensation
types who (especially if they are extraverts) only trust their own
senses, and gape in amazement at the intuitive's capacity to see
round corners or beneath the surface. Thomas the doubting
Apostle must have been one of these. And we certainly know the
people who are always running off on to some new track, forever
at the mercy of a new idea, who are incapable of dealing with
ordinary facts like catching trains or managing their money.
These are the intuitives, and sensation or a sense of reality is their
weakest point.

It is often easier to determine which is a person's fourth
undifferentiated function than which is his best. Our weakest
points are the ones which stand out. But if we can see the fourth,
the first can be arrived at by inference.

For instance, the man whose shocking lack of tact (which means
poor feeling) is his besetting sin, is likely to be predominantly a
thinking type. Or the one quite incapable of logical thought is
likely to function predominantly with feeling. The man who gets
stuck in a situation and can conceive of no possible way out is
probably a sensation type, whereas an intuitive is beset on all sides
by so many different possibilities that he has the greatest difficulty
in remaining in any situation at all.

The other day, for example, I watched with amazement an
intelligent original boy of fourteen trying to work out how many
exercise books of different colours he needed for the various subjects he was about to study at a new school. Blue for this subject,
green for that, and so on. But he was in difficulties. 'Can't you see,'
he said, 'that colours and numbers have no connection with one
another? They just don't add up.' This was an extreme case of
almost total lack of sensation function. There were so many possibilities, permutations and combinations between the colours and
the various subjects that it was well nigh impossible for the boy to
fix them. This boy is capable of clear thought. His feelings are
warm and reliable. So we can infer that his first function is intuition. This in fact accounts for his originality. Most original
thinkers are intuitives.

Now the only way of developing our lesser functions is to give
less energy to the first. This is no easy task, but we can learn to do
so. Certainly an analysis can help to the extent of developing the

c

second and third functions; but probably only the hard knocks of life itself can induce us to give up our best developed conscious function to the point of having enough available energy to dive down and reach our fourth.

Jung's theory of different psychological types is an invaluable aid because it helps us out of our habitual assumption that other people's minds work in the same way as our own. It was, I believe, an attempt to explain his own difference with Freud which set Jung off on this particular investigation.

In the degree to which a person is able consciously to use *all* his functions of thinking, feeling, sensation and intuition, he is liberated from the tyranny of any one of them and is able to use such function at any particular time as the situation demands — a far distant ideal which by no means appeals to all of us.

But knowing one's own type has another significance of enormous importance. It is through the inferior or fourth function that evil creeps in unawares. So if one knows which is one's inferior function one can more easily be on guard to see that it does not lead one wildly astray.

Our fourth function, being the one which is least within our conscious power to handle, is inevitably lit or touched in some way by the unconscious. When suddenly it comes to our aid it brings as it were the magic or mystical quality of the collective unconscious in its train. I am an intuitive, and I remember Jung once explained to me that I must not expect my fourth function, sensation, to be like the sensation of a sensation type. On the contrary, it would always appear to have a numinous quality. This is true. I have always despaired of mastering everyday reality with the same efficiency as other people I admire. At the same time matter, things, seem to behave much more oddly around me than they do with many of my friends. You see, to the intuitive it is the things of the senses which are magical not his intuitions which he takes as a matter of course.

On the other hand to the sensation type a sudden intuition appearing as it will out of the blue, lit by a glow from the unconscious, will seem heaven-sent. It may even be heaven-sent.

Similarly, if a feeling type, to whom thinking is of the utmost difficulty, is suddenly able to think something out, the result will appear with a luminous clarity; while the thinker whose feeling is touched will be overwhelmed by the force of his unexpected emotion. (Please remember that emotion is not identical with feeling or any other of the functions. Emotion always has its roots in the unconscious and manifests itself in the body.) The emotion of the thinker whose sympathy is aroused is likely to be far more overwhelming than that of the feeling type.

The case of Goebbels has been cited as a man whose feeling function was so faulty that he could connive at the extermination of millions of Jews, yet when his canary died he wept. Such sentimentality is not lack of feeling, but negative inferior feeling arising from the unconscious.

This brings me directly to the connection between evil and the fourth function. Goebbels had no adequate feeling function in consciousness with which to evaluate his monstrous deeds. Nor presumably had Hitler, nor any of his close collaborators. They knew what they were doing. Their thinking function enabled them to plan the crimes which served their ends. But they could not evaluate them consciously and correctly. The unconscious overwhelmed them through their inferior feeling and provided the terrific dynamism which enabled them to carry out their evil schemes.

Hitler prided himself on being guided solely by intuition. He treated his intuitions like commands of God. It is of course a fact that we all tend to treat our first function as though it had the authority of God. But Hitler was a house painter, and therefore probably a sensation type. If this is so then his intuition would be his fourth function which would explain its terrific force.

No intuition as a first conscious function could possibly have had the dynamism of Hitler's. His intuitions arose from the depths of the collective unconscious, alight with the flames of Hell. Hitler was a man possessed.

It was through his inferior or fourth undifferentiated function that evil did not creep but burst upon the world.

Baynes has pointed out that there may be such a thing as a national psychological type, and different nations tend to use one of their functions more consciously than the others.

He has pointed out that Germany is probably a thinking nation, and this is perhaps why the flames of Hitler's regime were able to spread throughout Germany. Lack of sound feeling opened the door to Germany's possession, and prevented the Germans from evaluating their deeds in all their horror. Germany is certainly a nation of philosophers, and has habitually been guided by philosophical principles. But, as thinkers, the feeling function of the Germans probably tends to be not a sound valuing of human life, but a combination of sentimentality and callous brutality.

The English, according to Baynes, are largely sensation types. Throughout history they have been the great colonizers because they knew how to handle facts. The areas they conquered were won neither in accordance with a principle nor out of any passionate love of country, but because they liked adventure and overcoming material obstacles. The British Empire was accumulated by accident.

Moreover England's diplomatic relations with other countries have continued to be a series of handling facts. That is why we are called perfidious Albion. We so often betray what other countries think must be our principles. In reality we have almost no principles to betray, so if one set of solutions does not work we simply try another.

Baynes has also pointed out that there is a very strong introverted feeling side to the English character, and this appears in the legend of King Arthur and the Knights of the Round Table. All clans tend to hold together by force of kinship, but the Arthurian Knights widened kinship to embrace humanity. Any man, woman or child in distress was their concern and could call upon them for succour. The spirit of the Arthurian legend has filtered down through the centuries, and appears daily in the Anglo-Saxon ideal of fair play. Fair play is not a rigid principle, it is not inexorable like justice: it is an essentially human feeling and is only concerned with essentially human values. British Common Law has been built up by past judges purely in the spirit of fair play. Fair play is a sign of a good feeling function.

But as recently as 1962, the British Government landed itself in an awkward dilemma. The Home Office granted the use of the platform of Trafalgar Square to the neo-Fascists, and refused it to the Campaign for Nuclear Disarmament.

In psychological terms what does this mean? Moseley, like Hitler, seemed to be lacking a feeling function. Racial injustice is repugnant to anyone capable of making a sound feeling judgment. It is anathema to our Arthurian traditional ideal of making all humanity our kin. Moreover, like Hitler, the Mosleyites seemed also to be possessed by inferior intuition. 'The blacks', they said, 'will completely override the whites. Send them back to

Africa. Let us keep England white. The Jews are the financiers of the world, they own all the armament factories, they thrive on and foster war. Down with the Jews!' — and so on. This is negative intuition, charged with fear arising from the unconscious through the inferior function, and it lies at the root of the neo-Fascist movement.

This ill-developed fourth function is the gateway through which evil might once more try to explode its way. We have here a problem with no easy solution. To refuse a platform to the neo-Fascists could drive them underground where they would be still more dangerous. And yet officially to permit the public preaching of race hatred seems as irresponsible as allowing a dangerous drug to be put on the market. On the other hand it may be a risk we have to take.

The case of the Campaign for Nuclear Disarmament is almost the opposite. The scientist's two supreme functions are brilliant intuition combined with thought. To give his ideas tangible shape the scientist also needs to use his sensation. But feeling, the judgment and appraisal of human values, can easily be dispensed with. It would appear to be through the ill-developed feeling function that the world is threatened by Russia and China and even the United States. Indeed, lack of feeling function seems to be a general malady. England, too, is apparently throwing over her native feeling and guiding herself more and more by her inferior thinking — and therefore throwing overboard her ability to act as a brake in the suicidal arms race.

Those who campaign for Nuclear Disarmament are fully aware of man's danger and are public-spirited enough to concern themselves with fighting for man's survival. We may or may not agree with them, but there is no question of psychic contagion as there is with the neo-Fascists. To ban the bomb at the moment may be impracticable. It may even be unwise, but this is a matter of opinion. It is possible that the feeling of these campaigners, which puts the survival of humanity before all else, may be misled by poor thinking, so that they may in fact bring war nearer by misleading the Russians or Chinese into a false belief that we will never fight. But Bertrand Russell could hardly be accused of poor thinking.

How can we decide to which protagonist we should lend our weight? I can see neither principle nor psychological validity underlying the refusal of Trafalgar Square to the Nuclear

Disarmers. Their rejection was of course a matter of expedience —
the sensation function at work on the part of the British Government and the Police: a tactic to delay the impact of their
protest.

These movements which I have described in Trafalgar Square,
are of course in the outer world generally. They are probably
outer manifestations of an inner movement which we can
understand if we look at the Archetype of the Eternal
Youth.[1]

Puer Aeternus is the name given to those many young men
today who seem overly endowed and inspired as youths, yet do not
grow into what is normally considered responsible adult citizens.
They remain at heart, and often in behaviour, eternally young.
They may be artists, poets, airmen, scientists or 'angry young
men'. Their main characteristic is that one feels that they are
permeated with and activated by some spirit of an outstanding
quality. We have all met them and easily recognize them in
our midst. They have their counterpart among young women
also.

Hitherto psychologists have tended to regard these young
people as immature Peter Pans who cannot grow up, men and
women with mother complexes. Treat them and they will with
any luck take up the responsibilities of life in a normal way. Very
often they do so but not uncommonly at the price of losing their
spiritual gifts. They may even swing to the opposite extreme of
utter banality.

The apparent increasing number of these young men and
women today is evidence of an inner happening. Organized religion has become fossilized, which inhibits the spiritual transformation necessary to keep pace with man's development. The
fossilization of religion goes hand in hand with the police state.
The archetype of spiritual renewal is finding its way not within the
churches but through the individual young men and women of
whom I am speaking. They are the channels along which a new
spiritual awareness is trying to break through. They are in fact
activated and possessed by the archetype of spiritual renewal.
Their danger is that they do not always know what has got into
them and may identify with the archetype itself. They then think

[1] I owe this to a brilliant lecture by Marie Louise Van Franz addressed
to the Congress of the International Association of Analytical Psychology
on 'The Archetype of the Puer Aeternus'.

they have the monopoly of this new spiritual awareness, often believing themselves to be prophets or saviours.

To be identified with an archetype is one of man's most common but most acute perils, and it is not unusual for these inspired youths to break down and land in mental hospitals. In these cases evil has crept in through the fourth function. Not through its dynamism, as with the neo-Fascists, but through its almost total lack. Reality sense is absent.

If only these people could understand that they are being used by the archetype of renewal, as we all are in any moment of inspiration, but that it is essential to avoid identifying with it, many personal catastrophes might be avoided. Indeed holding fast to their own individual intuitive gifts, at the same time as they keep their feet on the ground of reality, is a spiritual achievement of unique service to mankind. By so doing within themselves the new spiritual awakening has a chance of filtering through to mankind as a whole.

On the whole the menace to civilization today seems to come from man's over-developed thinking, and the consequent unadaptedness of his fourth function, feeling, which thereby lets in the evil. His feeling brings with it all the dynamic forces of the unconscious, good and bad — its courage and inspiration, but also its terror — which makes us pile armament upon armament, hydrogen bomb on hydrogen bomb.

This terror 'gets us all in the night', and the weakest of us fly for succour to the doctors. Unfortunately their remedy is often to calm anxiety at all costs. Even the ordinary discomforts of pregnancy must be relieved. On the face of it, to relieve anxiety with tranquillizers so that people can carry on with their ordinary business may seem to be a boon to the suffering individual. A tranquillizer in a moment of crisis may be essential. But what happens to the anxiety thus suppressed? Is it not mounting up in the unconscious with ever increasing magnitude and momentum till one day it will be forced to explode?

It is not when we are feeling cheerful and complacent, but when we are in the throes of distress that we pray. Similarly it is not our lightness of heart but our distress which gives us the impetus to seek our inmost truth. Too much medical tranquillizing may actually cheat the more sensitive among us from becoming whole.

Jung maintains that our only hope of holding the blind, hysterical

masses in check is for enough people to contain the opposites
within themselves instead of either swinging violently from the one
extreme to the other, or projecting the undesirable opposite upon
an outer enemy. We do not yet know the extent to which a relatively few integrated individuals can break the force of a rising
storm; but their impetus is not that of numerical superiority, nor
in the field of action, their healing effect is in the unconscious
which we all share.

To have the use of all four functions means to have an ego
which is in no danger of being submerged by the unconscious through an ill-developed fourth function, or a possession
by some partial aspect of ourselves. It means rather to be
in touch with that vital centre of ourselves, which Jung calls the
Self. It is this centre, not our active little egos, which effects the
healing.

To accept one's own personal shadow means to accept responsibility for its behaviour, not necessarily the licence to live and
put in practice all we find within — this is a common fallacy. It
demands not only self-knowledge but the utmost vigilance to see it
does not break out unawares. And if it should, to call it back and
make amends and admit very humbly that this unruly shadow is a
bit of me.

What one does, one is. Not what one says nor thinks one is, but
what one does. Doing may be a concern of an inner invisible
process which we call being, but it is still what in fact one does;
though, of course, the quality of our being will depend on the
value of our actions or our influence.

It may sometimes be wisdom to use one's shadow deliberately.
Anger is a shadow quality in our well-behaved society, but consciously directed it can move mountains. I once saw a small boy
aged four rush angrily up to a Spanish mule-driver shouting, 'I
won't have you beat the mules like that.' The man stopped, utterly
taken aback, and turning to the couple of men behind him,
ordered sheepishly, 'Master Johnny says we are not to beat the
mules.' On that occasion at least the mules carried out their heavy
work free from blows owing to the anger on the part of a small
child, spontaneously but correctly used.

Christ vented his anger on the moneylenders in the temple. He
knew what he was doing. We also need to know what we are
doing, as it is only when our shadow comes up unbeknown that it
causes mischief.

Hardness of heart is another shadow quality, and the people who are hard in life without knowing and without intention may cause much misery for others and themselves. Yet there are moments when use of one's hard, unyielding shadow is the one thing necessary to save the situation. We need at times to use our shadow, but never to be its victim.

It is only if we are truly centred that we can be trusted to use our shadow qualities spontaneously in the right time and place. 'When the wrong man does the right thing it will turn out wrong' says the Chinese saying, 'and when the right man does the wrong thing it will turn out right.' To be the right man requires more than consciousness. It requires to be centred.

Life insists on being lived, and anything that belongs to one's life which is allowed to lie dormant has to be lived by someone else. If we do not accept our shadow we force our children to carry the burden of our undeveloped capacities. They may become mediocre scientists or artists because we denied our own talents. They may become doctors, which they are not suited to be, because we failed to use our innate capacity for healing, or inept politicians to fulfil our unlived ambitions.

Our interconnection does not end with the family. We all meet in the unconscious. How many men have been hanged for murder merely because they were the weak recipients of the murderous shadow of the whole race? There would be fewer murders if we could all acknowledge within ourselves how easy it would be for anyone of us to kill. In wartime we explain our brutality some other way. In peacetime we forget and some man or woman slightly weaker than the rest is hanged virtually for us.

I will write at greater length of woman's bright shadow in another chapter, but I cannot close this one without speaking of woman's direst and most destructive shadow. The witch is chiefly woman's responsibility. All women who have not totally lost contact with the unconscious are in touch with power. Power is not necessarily bad. Its direction is what makes it good or bad.

The life force which surges up through women is a tremendous power, whether employed biologically or in some other way. We have heard a great deal about woman's suffocating quality. She pours out energy on those for whom she cares and does not know she suffocates. Giving feels like love, but giving without measure and without discrimination stifles.

It is when a woman actually uses the power with which the feminine is in contact for her own personal ends that she becomes truly a witch. This is real evil which needs all our resourcefulness to fight. I suspect there are few women who will not find a witch lurking somewhere within themselves if only they dig deep enough.

But I think that a woman will also turn witch today for other reasons than personal power. The deeply buried feminine in us whose concern is the unbroken connection of all growing things is in passionate revolt against the stultifying, life-destroying, anonymous machine of the civilization we have built. She is consumed by an inner rage which is buried in a layer of the unconscious often too deep for us to recognize. She becomes destructive of anything and everything, sometimes violently but often by subtle passive obstruction.

I believe it is often this inner protest which breaks out in neurotic illness, in sensitive men as well as in women; or turns destructive in places where it was not intended. With more consciousness, feminine anger could be harnessed to a creative end.

I have touched on three levels of responsibility. In the outer world it is imperative, for the sake of peace, that we see our own dark shadow and admit that it is ours, instead of projecting it on to other countries.

But ultimately our most far-reaching contribution lies on a deeper level in the carrying of our own individual shadows, dark and bright. Dark shadows, once conscious, can to some extent at least be curbed from causing mischief, and their dynamism can be redirected. Our bright shadows of dormant potentialities are obviously also needed both for ourselves and for the welfare of the whole.

Deepest of all lies the feminine shadow. Above all, I appeal to women to find the shadow within themselves, not only the destructive power-demon witch, but also their own peculiarly feminine spiritual quality of which we seem equally unaware. This exists today also in men, but wherever it may dwell it needs a voice.

Our personal responsibility for the outer world may seem infinitesimal — indeed it is. But taking individual responsibility for our own personal shadow, dark and bright, is a small attainable achievement, though it demands a lifetime's determination and a lifetime's courage. And as we are all connected beneath the surface, our little individual pebbles of consciousness may send ripples to the furthest shore.

# III

# *Man the Hero*

TWO YEARS AGO a couple of boys who live on opposite sides of my road rigged up a private telephone between the two houses. Even their parents were thrilled when the toy catapult actually carried their wire from roof to roof. This phone, quite illegal of course, has been in constant use ever since, saving the parents, incidentally, quite a lot in telephone bills.

One day the two boys, by then about fourteen, came home from a jaunt in town in a state of great jubilation. 'We have been doing a swop with the telephone company,' they said, and proudly showed a new telephone mouthpiece. 'How do you mean "swapped"?' inquired the parents. 'Well, we've got this in exchange for our old one which wasn't working very well.' Parents began to look anxious. 'But who gave it to you?' 'Oh, no one *gave* it to us,' they replied with scorn, 'we took this mouthpiece from a public telephone box and fitted up ours instead. It works allright,' they added, 'we tried, to make sure. You see the public telephones work with a stronger current than ours so they can afford to have a weak apparatus. It won't make any difference to them but it will make a lot of difference to us.'

The parents were by that time in the constant quandary of parents: how to show disapproval without being so damping that they will never hear of future exploits. They managed with skill and adroitness.

To me this incident was a godsend. I suddenly realized how fine is the line between heroism and delinquency. These boys had carried out a skilled operation in full view of the public. The thrill of danger far outweighed in their minds any sense of moral disapproval. I had to admit that I should have enjoyed the exploit myself. These boys clearly had it in them to become delinquents — or heroes, and which it would be, depended very largely on the kind of challenges life offered. These boys' cultural future is adequate to turn them into heroes. But boys who are kept throughout their adolescent years seated at school desks in a state of boredom, trying to evade learning matters in which they have no interest, are thwarted of any challenge whatsoever. By the time they leave school the desire to achieve has been stifled in most of them.

However, the stronger and more imaginative ones will still be impelled to some form of audacious action. Heroes they *must* be. Without some form of heroism a man hardly feels himself to be a man. It is the hero in man which makes him really male.

Our delinquents, of whom society complains so bitterly and so complacently, are the failed heroes — the ones who tried and couldn't find the right channel. Better rob a train than be a nobody. Better prove one's prowess in a gang war than remain an anonymous fool. Even rapes and murders surely have their original impulse in the need to be a hero.

This hero impulse in man needs to be better understood, if we are not to make serious mistakes. This was demonstrated, remember, in an alleged spy trial in 1963, where heroism was mistaken for delinquency. An Italian atomic physicist was arrested and tried for preparing to give secrets to the Russians. He was not in secret work and had no secrets to give. But as the story unfolded at the trial it became obvious that here was a man who was fascinated by danger. He had been in the Italian Resistance during the war, and so had been trained to act alone on his own initiative against the enormous odds of an organized army. The accused explained at the trial that he had hoped by going along with the Russians, accepting their information of how to pass them secrets, and their gadgets which would enable him to do so, that he might in the end uncover the intricacies of their spy ring for the benefit of the British Government. The prosecutor and the judge poured scorn on the likelihood of so intelligent a man being such a fool as to think he could fight the Russians single-handed. This man's life hung in the balance for a fortnight on the court's understanding or failure to understand the significance of the hero archetype. Mercifully the jury showed some insight, and in face of the clearest possible direction by the judge to convict, had the courage to acquit the accused on every count.

Now in what lies the significance of the hero archetype in man? It is probably at the root of his emergence from the level of the animal kingdom. It is his particular instinctual drive which has enabled him to overcome the obstacles of nature, enlarge his knowledge and utilize Nature's energies and secrets for his own purposes. Every new mastery over the resources of the earth, every new penetration, whether into outer space or into the mysteries of the atom, is an achievement of heroes. This impulse to overcome danger and difficulties is built into the structure of man's psyche, and evidence of the pattern is clear enough even in little details.

But heroism is not limited to man's prowess against external odds. Going hand in hand with these has been man's heroic fight for consciousness. It is this struggle which is depicted over and over again in mythology. The hero with a thousand faces is always the same hero-consciousness. The struggle for consciousness is the perennial struggle of the son to break free from the Great Mother. The degree of our consciousness and our conscious control over our lives is illusory. Man's ego, which he has evolved with such labour over the ages, is far less strong than we like to think it. And the drive towards consciousness demands all man's heroic qualities. It is one long wrestle, already lasting for millennia — and still going on — a wrestle whose outcome is by no means assured.

I have seen even children training themselves to face danger. On the dark landing at the top of my stairs in Spain, my children used to imagine a lion lurking under a settee, and I watched the genuine terror on their faces as they ran downstairs to the lighted hall. But no sooner had they reached safety than they crept upstairs to taunt the lion all over again. They needed to face fear.

This was a tiny repetition of a constant psychic pattern. You may recall the legend of Theseus who insisted, against all the wishes and contrivances of the king his father, on being one of the twelve men and maidens who were chosen to face the Minotaur. His destiny demanded that he should be a hero and slay the dreaded monster.

The spirit of David the shepherd-boy who single-handed slew Goliath, still lurks beneath man's skin. The history of man is one long procession of heroes overthrowing tyrants, even old divinities, stretching from Prometheus who stole fire from the Gods, to such civilized protests against tradition as the Bishop of Woolwich's best-seller, *Honest to God.*

We have come some way since the days when men had to summon their energies to hunt or go to war by means of ritual dance. We have learned to focus our energies so that we can pursue an outer goal or a line of thought with some continuity, and without sinking back into lethargy. But lethargy is always just round the corner, and politicians still have to beat their drums in modern journalistic fashion to make us go to war.

However, man has unquestionably emerged from a state of tribal consciousness to that of the responsible individual. But the process is so precarious that it appears to be in danger of tipping over into its opposite of a new form of collectivity.

Man has climbed up from the Great Mother of the collective unconscious, but he is falling inadvertently into the Great Mother of the affluent society whose nurse is the welfare state. He has become little more than a number. His skill is required less and less as the machines take over. His personal responsibility is diminished the greater our organizations grow. He has been sucked back into a different kind of collectivity and is in the same peril as the child who had begun to emerge as an individual personality but has withdrawn. He is in danger of becoming an idiot, an idiot disguised as a well-dressed efficient automaton.

To meet this danger a new kind of hero is needed. We do not lack the heroism which makes men risk their lives encircling the earth or facing journeys to the moon. Our daily press is full of outer heroism. Not long ago, no fewer than seven men offered to go down a narrow tube two hundred feet below the surface of the earth to help rescue miners trapped in a flooded mine. Even a child will risk its life to save another. But in our extraverted modern world we have become so oriented outwards that the inner world with its living images, its treasures and its terrors, has for the most part been forgotten. We have repressed our natural fears of the inner world and in so doing we have projected our fear on to some outer political enemy: or some sinister figure of our acquaintance.

We no longer have a Medicine Man who will probe the secrets of the unconscious for us and protect us with his ritual magic. The Churches which shielded us in the past have lost their power to do so. The danger from the unconscious, by which we are in fact threatened all the time, has been reasoned out of existence, with the result that paranoia has become a common complaint (almost as rife as the common cold).

My subject is 'Man the Hero'. Now does this mean man as distinct from woman or does it mean mankind? I think it means man. It unquestionably is the male of the human race who is the active partner and has explored the greatness of the earth and the heavens and the smallness of invisible particles. It is also he who became conscious first and has, as a result, been the architect of modern culture.

The consciousness of woman is a very recent acquisition:

> While Eve lay sleeping
> Man awoke
> And clambered on her breasts
>
> Poised on their towering
> Domes he reached
> Beyond the Night
>
> From her lifted knees
> Far leaping
> Grasped the light
> While Eve lay sleeping.

Today woman is sleeping no longer, with the uneasy results we see all around us. Gender seems to be confused. One is no longer quite sure whether women are feminine, nor how far men are male.

But the emancipation of women came about through their finding a hero within themselves. It was this which overcame all obstacles in their path: the law, tradition, the obscurantism of their own as well as of the other sex.

The change in woman's attitude towards the hero in the last fifty years is very marked. Before the First World War it was men's business to be heroes. Women had assumed that men fought while women wept. The harridans who presented men in mufti with white feathers were only an extreme expression of woman's general unconscious assumption that man was of course a hero, and if he was not, there must be something wrong with him. Women in fact projected on to men their own unconscious cowardice as well as their own latent heroism.

In the interval between the two Great Wars, however, women won a great part of their battle for equality. In doing so they found that they too could stand up against outer odds and were quite capable of being heroes themselves, and by the time the Second World War broke out women were prepared to take their part alongside the men.

From then on there is no doubt about it that the new generations

D

of women have also shared with the men a new leap forward of consciousness. The young people today of both sexes seem to have started off on a level of awareness to which their parents had only painfully and pantingly arrived.

None the less, although woman no longer projects her own latent hero on to her men folk, which of course in the past did actually help the men to be heroes, she does not appear to have outgrown her old expectation that a hero is what he ought to be.

So the poor man suffers doubly. No longer boosted by the women on the one hand, and actually competed with by them on the other, he feels depotentiated and unable to rise to the heights expected of him. All this at the same time as he is rightfully developing his own more sensitive feminine side.

One constantly meets the gentle understanding man, without an ounce of hero in him, the source of quite unreasonable exasperation on the part of his wife who has not yet realized that modern men for the most part just are not heroes, and have no more reason or aptitude for heroism than she. She has to learn that if it is a hero she wants she had better find him within herself.

In his essay on 'Modern Women in Europe' Jung says that man can go no further in the pursuit of consciousness until woman catches up with him. This was written before the Second World War, and since then she has been very busy catching up. But her task is a double one since she has to develop her own masculine ability to focus, before she is able to throw her new found light on to her own mysterious nature and make this conscious also.

The first part of this task is similar to that of the mythological masculine hero who has to free himself from the Great Mother by achieving an ego, a will of his own. This step woman has already partially taken but she now finds herself in new danger of blindly accepting man's values as though they were her own.

A new act of heroism is needed before she can delve into her own feminine nature and salvage her own feminine values. Even in those cases (comparatively rare) where she has done this and knows what her true values are, she still has before her the enormous task of holding to her true self with firmness so that her values begin to permeate society and check or alter the disastrous course of materialistic progress and over-population on which we are hurling ourselves pell mell.

The heroism of men is still turned to outer space. All honour to their imagination, their skill in wresting the secrets from nature,

and above all to their incredible courage. But one cannot help
wondering if man's pursuit of the physical moon is not the outer
counterpart of his paramount need, of which he is not yet fully
aware, to explore the cold unpredictable half-light of his own
feminine nature.

Modern education is not conducive to the emergence of heroes
in any field other than that of scientific discovery and the conquest
of outer space.

We need a new kind of hero. We have always had reformers
who would fight against the evils of society, but, with the general
collective depersonalization of society, our reformers have become
impersonal associations such as the 'Association for the Abolition
of this, that or the other.' There is not much room for personal
heroism here. We rely on the static weight of numbers rather than
on the far more dynamic hero archetype.

But the sphere where the hero archetype can still have full play
is within the individual himself. It requires all the qualities of a
hero to turn from the pleasant harmless 'persona' mask which one
has so carefully cultivated, and which one really believed one was,
to find the elements of cruelty within oneself of which one had no
idea. One may even find a full-blown sadistic tyrant, such as could
have been a very efficient governor of a concentration camp had
circumstances placed one in Hitler's Germany.

Or one may discover beneath the most well meant and generous
gestures, a witch who is busy plotting in the shadows to achieve
her own power-inspired ends. Here, within, is where evil can be
adequately met.

There are inner heroes too. One can recognize the hero in
modern young men and women of a particular indefinable
spiritual quality. They are the visionaries who refuse to lose their
vision and yet do manage to live in the materialistic world in
which they find themselves, holding the opposites together within
them rather than going out as preachers or reformers.

This is an enormously difficult task today, the opposites are so
far apart. These incipient heroes often fail. Again and again we
see a young man, or woman, with a light in the eyes which illumines as well as sees. Yet again and again as the exigencies of life
crowd in on them the light fades and they settle down to the rat
race of competing with the Joneses, indistinguishable from all the
other rats.

More tragic, and no less a loss, are the visionaries who have been overwhelmed, whether by the incandescence of the vision or the suffocating menace of society. These break down. Their vision is treated as an illness, neither valued nor understood. There is no attempt to canalize its energy. It is regarded as an illness to be cured.

Only a few achieve the colossal task of holding together, without being split asunder, the clarity of their vision alongside an ability to take their place in a materialistic world.

These are the modern heroes. All the more are they heroes for not being recognized as such. Some are invisible, the struggle fought unobserved. Some openly shrug their shoulders at the disapproval of their fellows, refusing to deviate one hair's breadth from their standpoint, though the invisibility of their goal makes them victims of misunderstanding and taunts of being escapists.

Among the ranks of these are the artists, poets, musicians, painters. Artists have at least a form within which they can hold their own conflicting opposites together. But there are some who have no recognized artistic form to serve this purpose. They are artists of living. To my mind these last are the supreme heroes in our soulless society.

Robert Frost describes such a one in a poem entitled:

### Escapist — Never

He is no fugitive — escaped, escaping,
No one has seen him stumble looking back,
His fear is not behind him but beside him
On either hand to make his course perhaps
A crooked straightness yet no less a straightness.
He runs face forward. He is a pursuer,
He seeks a seeker who in his turn seeks
Another still, lost far into the distance.
Any who seek him seek in him the seeker.
His life is a pursuit of a pursuit forever.
It is the future that creates his present,
He is an interminable chain of longing.

# IV

# *Roles of Women—Woman as Mediator*

THE HERO ARCHETYPE pertains specially to masculine psychology. Being a woman myself I am particularly interested in the psychology of women and am constantly wondering how far they have legitimately different roles to play in life from that of men.

Many of my contemporaries maintain that there is little difference between the working of a man's or woman's mind and that it is only in their biological function that they play different roles. Simone de Beauvoir is one of these. To her it is only their education and the assumptions of their parents which creates an illusory distinction.

My own view is just the opposite. It is based not on theory but on personal observation. Moreover the many years I have lived in Spain, which, in many respects, is still a matriarchal country, have perhaps given me more direct contact with the unconscious of woman than I could easily have had in England.

We are certainly living in an age in which it is increasingly difficult to speak of the different characteristics of man and woman. Women are fast developing their masculine side and more and more men are in touch with the feminine in themselves. None the less, women are still basically feminine and men basically masculine, so I shall speak of man and woman and ask you to remember that what I say may not necessarily fit any particular case. I can only speak of conditions in the West and more particularly of the conditions prevailing in England.

At the close of the period of rationalism which led up to the First World War many of us, shocked at the Armageddon which appeared to have been the result of a masculine culture, really believed that if women took their place in the control of affairs the world would *ipso facto* become a pleasanter place, and that their influence would stop wars and make civilization more humane.

Forty years later we look around with dismay. Women have
penetrated every field of society, but the world in which we live is
more, not less, tormented.

Men's often heard criticism that though women are successfully
vying with them in every field, they lack creative imagination is, I
believe, on the whole a fair one. They lack the spirit of adventure,
the generous willingness to sacrifice self for a cause, which has
always been such a notable characteristic of the male. Have
women, I wonder, carried into the world at large their feminine
limitation of outlook which has concerned itself from time immemorial with the individual relationships of a woman to her man and
to her children? *Her* children and *her* man. Women do not readily
bother about Vietnamese children or the horror of concentration
camps unless they actually *see* them.

The greatest lovers of humanity have nearly all been
men — Christ, St. Francis, Gandhi. With few exceptions the great
women of history — Joan of Arc, St. Teresa, Florence Nightingale, Elizabeth Fry, Nurse Cavell — have been blessed with a
good proportion of masculinity. They could not possibly have
done what they did without.

Women have permeated man's world, but, instead of re-
generating it, they seem to have contaminated it with their own
pettiness of outlook, with the sublime indifference of a tree which
is concerned with its own growth, and its own acorns, caring
nothing, for it knows nothing, of the forest as a whole.

At the same time the greater preponderance of the feminine in
man's psyche today no doubt also contributes to this state of
affairs. Just as the masculinity in women is apt to be less creative
than that of men, so also the femininity in man is less concerned
with the values of life and relationship than the femininity of
woman. He tends to adopt her softness rather than her strength,
her vanity rather than her capacity to give.

The tendency in both men and women to take over the less vital
characteristics of the other sex and, in so doing, to lose touch with
their own fundamental truth is, I believe, a transitional one, but in
the meantime it has a disastrous effect. Many women have forgotten, in the modern emphasis on a career and economic independence, that woman has a role to play towards man which is
inherent in her nature, a role which is not a sharing of his intellectual interests nor the providing of his meals; not becoming the
mother of his children nor being his sexual partner; but over and

beyond all these, her role is still, as it always has been, to be a mediator to man of his own creative inspirations, a channel whereby the riches of the unconscious can flow to him more easily than if she were not there.

At present it is the young men who appear most unsure of themselves, not the young women. Men feel threatened in their masculine role because women are now competing, but do not yet know what is the next step in their own evolution.

The young women, on the other hand, are still buoyed up by the exhilaration of their newly found status. They continue to be wives and mothers, yet are successful in man's world as well. But in so doing they often fail to realize how precarious men feel, and how much the particular man needs his woman to believe in him and to welcome his vision with as much warmth and tenderness as she accepts his child.

He looks to her for recognition of his unique personalness. He does not want to be merely the man about the house, the husband whose duty it is to earn money, and wash up after supper. Perhaps man's need is to be trusted even more than to be understood. He needs to be believed in, and his work, whether she understands it or not, to be given full value.

But he needs her also to *express* herself. Herself. It is her own deepest self that he must know, not her opinions which she has picked up from parents, schools and the daily press, but her *deepest* self. How many women can give him that?

To be a true mediator to the masculine, whether it be an actual man or the masculine in herself, requires not speech but consciousness on the part of the woman. Over and over again one sees the increased consciousness of a woman influencing her man, with no words said. Language can falsify by its very precision. Clever conversation does not make a relationship. True communion happens in the silence.

Yet to be fully conscious *herself*, a woman needs to be able to make some formulation in words. One does not really completely know what one cannot express at all, and most women are incredibly inarticulate about the things which matter to them most; though, curiously enough, the more educated they are the less they seem to be aware of this fact.

Unfortunately, most women do not realize how little they express their true selves. They talk in slogans, adopt man's principles without his flexibility, and fight man's causes without man's charity. There is nothing so ruthless as a woman with a cause between her teeth.

It looks to me as though we are caught in a dichotomy. On the one hand women are educated to accept man's values blindly. Schools and colleges have grown up throughout the centuries to meet the needs of growings boys, and girls have fitted themselves into what was already there. They have accepted without question the masculine over-valuation of a thinking function and of physical prowess. Girls have adopted the ability to do mathematics as the test of intelligence and a capacity for games as the criterion of bodily perfection. Many an inferiority complex stems from these mistakes.

On the other hand, women on the whole are more biologically minded than they care to recognize, which undermines their modern education.

The vast majority of women are still willy-nilly housewives and mothers, and for the sake of the children born and yet unborn they want security and material comfort and the status quo. With her new found power, woman has become the hub around which society revolves. It is not her vote but her purchasing power which counts. The advertizing agencies know and exploit this fact. It is she who pushes up the material standards of living, seeking ever-new gadgets to ease her burden of overwork, not noticing that in doing so she is binding her husband's feet more firmly to the crippling treadmill he detests in order to meet time payments and the monthly bills. Her panacea is always more gadgets, not more simplicity.

Over-worked she certainly is, but how often she has failed to understand the nature of man's malaise or to see how heavy is the burden she loads on him. She is blissfully unaware of her failure to give him what he needs. Her achievement of becoming a creative being in her own right and a factor of importance in the economic world, is of little avail if she deprives man of her fundamental role of helping him to find himself. To do this she must never lose her natural contact with the living springs in the unconscious. This is her direct responsibility.

The parable of the wise virgins who kept oil ready in their lamps for the coming of the bridegroom expresses, I believe, the basis of feminine spirituality.

One must have lived near the Mediterranean to feel the deep significance of oil. It is pressed with hard labour from the bitter inedible olive, fruit of a wild tree which has been drastically pruned. It is plunged into deep water to be purified, and when it rises to the surface clear and greenish-gold it becomes a staple food and fuel for light. It is not for nothing that kings are anointed with oil, for it is a symbol of spiritual transformation. This is the oil that women need to keep ever ready in their lamps.

To do so is an attitude of mind. It is the readiness for relationship in whatever field, whether it be with God, another human being, a work of art, a blackbird's song, or with one's own inner masculine counterpart. It is a readiness of the feminine soul for the meeting with another, though that other may be her own creative spirit.

Her task is two-fold. If she fails to have oil always ready in her lamp for the actual man, she fails him in the essential role he asks of her. But it is more than this. The oil is her feminine spirituality in the totality of her own psyche. It expresses an attitude of spiritual waiting, and tending, and readiness for the meeting with its opposite which is a prerequisite for inner wholeness.

Without this she becomes a prey to the masculine within herself, a raging spirit of intellectual or physical activity to which no man can be related, and to which she can in no way relate herself. She is a woman possessed.

But if she can hold the oil ready within the lamp, then, when the masculine spark comes, there burns a flame which is alive, and lights our human world.

This flame is Love. Love is wholly beyond us. It alights upon us and illumines our lives *only* when the opposites meet. Love may be born of the meeting between living creatures, or it may shine from within any human being, born of his or her own inner wholeness. It is equally in man or woman where the masculine and feminine meet, but the inner wholeness of men would, I believe, become less difficult if we women could remember to play our part.

It is primarily women who need to keep in contact with the springs of life, with the inseparable connection of all growing things and their eternal continuity: spring, summer, autumn and winter, followed eternally by another spring.

On every level death is the forerunner of life renewed. There is no birth without a prior death. The acorn dies for the emergence of the oak. At the birth of the baby the maiden dies to become a mother. In regions of the mind every new idea rings the death

knell of ideas out-worn. In the life of the spirit, only through death
can there be immortality.

In the book Jung wrote with Kerenyi[1] he points out the essential awareness of continuity between mothers and daughters:

> We could say that every mother contains her daughter in
> herself and every daughter her mother, and every woman
> extends backwards into her mother and forwards into her
> daughter. This participation and inter-mingling give rise to that
> particular uncertainty as regards time; a woman lives earlier as
> a mother, later as a daughter. The conscious experience of these
> ties produces the feeling that her life is spread out over gener-
> ations. The first step towards the immediate experience and
> conviction of being outside time, brings with it a feeling of
> immortality.

I suspect that when women lose their contact with this underlying feeling of immortality they undermine the sense of purpose
and worth-whileness of life for men as well. Man in his rationality
may have relied on women to retain their hold on the irrational
until he could find it for himself. What, oh what, have we done in
blindly following him into the strictly rational?

The tragedy of today is that civilization in the West has gone too
far in the direction of masculine separation and the masculine
urge to discover and create for its own sake and the accompanying
danger that women are throwing over their sense of cosmic
awareness and the connection of all growing things in order
to adopt men's values in their stead. That only serves to
upset the necessary balance between the opposite poles. It is
now imperative for men and women alike to stretch from pole
to pole in order to achieve the paradox of holding both attitudes
at once.

I have tried to describe in a little poem the contribution of the
feminine side when woman's own conscious masculine discrimination has freed it from being a stifling jungle or a submerging sea.
It is the contribution that the spiritual feminine has to offer to the
masculine world, and the individual woman to the individual
man.

[1] C. G. Jung and C. Kerenyi, *Essays on a Science of Mythology*, Princeton
University Press.

## The Water She Brings

Water, dancing to break the light
Into a million colours.
Water mirroring the flight
Of circling birds.
A pool, guarded by tall trees,
Waiting for him to dive and salve
The drowning stars.
Water for parched lips, unfailing
And water for the moon to trace the path
Of his last sailing.

Now do all women play this mediating role? And what really does it mean to be a mediator?

To mediate is to be a connecting link between two things. To begin with, what are the two things or states between which woman is supposed to stand, holding out a hand to each as it were, helping them to come to terms? We can think of mediators in any field. Let us begin at the circumference of our lives and work inwards, seeing at which levels women do in fact play this mediator's role.

On the world stage mediation between conflicting powers or opposing ideologies is often called for. I have not noticed that women take any particular part. In such spheres as these, women as yet seldom play any role at all, for in the realm of ideas and power politics women as women have not learned to function. There are occasional exceptions but on the whole they join the ranks of men adding their moral weight to his through numbers, not through any different quality of being.

The same is true within our nation states. Industrial disputes, the quarrels of political parties, dissension between rival churches, show no sign of any woman's mediation to soften their bitterness. There are associations of women's groups but I doubt if they do more than exacerbate the situation.

The first glimmer of any such thing as real mediation appears within the schools, and that but sparsely. The child who finds a teacher that can actually help him pass from childhood into the adult world is fortunate, for teachers who have the gift of standing halfway between a child's mind and that of an adult are rare, and they are just as likely to be men as women, perhaps even more likely. The ones I happen to have known have all been men.

Drawing our circle closer we come to the family, and here at last we arrive at the fundamental, archetypal pattern in which we are all nurtured, where father is Father and mother, Mother.

What does this mean? In actual fact it is often all mixed up and mother's animus frequently plays the role of Father, wielding the stick of authority over children and husband alike; while the children run, not to her, when they are hurt, but to father.

None the less it is here, within the family, that woman has, in outer life, her first real opportunity to play her role of mediator.

When father is in fact Father he stands for law and order and authority, and the big world outside. He can lead the children to respect and obey its forms, and finally to take their place in adult society.

But the world is harsh and wholly unpredictable to the child who has only half emerged from the mists and timelessness of the great unconscious. Fiery dragons are far easier to deal with than irate grown-ups. In the boundless realm of fantasy one can take a sword and kill the smoking monster, emerging as the hero. Even if the giant enemy is too strong, or has a hide too thick for one's small sword to penetrate, one can always render oneself invisible, or spread one's wings and fly over his head with a mocking laugh and sail away to the next adventure.

In the prosaic world of everyday a mocking laugh is more likely to produce a scolding. How bewildering a child's life must be. He is assailed on both sides by two completely different sets of values.

When already in my forties I had a dream which most aptly described the predicament of my own childhood, or that of any other small child caught between these opposing worlds: *In the dream I was a shy little girl aged six* (I was in fact a shy little girl) *who went to visit the House of Lords. I opened the door and crept in. There they all were in a large square hall, dressed in black and all jabbering at once in Latin. I was much too small for them to notice me so I slipped round the edge of the hall and up the great wide stairs to an imposing gallery where sat still more rows of black clothed men. I looked round carefully. Yes, there he was, the man I was looking for, the Archbishop of Canterbury. I ran towards him and flung myself upon his neck weeping with a cry of protest: 'But the Queen doesn't believe in God!'*

Indeed she could not believe in the God of these black clothed Latin-mumbling men, for the picture of the queen, full-sized before my eyes, was not that of the reigning Queen Victoria, nor of my own mother, but a glowing colourful Queen of Hearts.

Heart and intellect had different gods even at the age of six, and the child was in tears in her bewilderment. I woke from that dream in actual tears.

Heart and intellect, love and thought, the poetry of mystical insight and prosaic reality, No. 1 and No. 2 personalities, were all opposites, hardly on speaking terms.

How badly the child needs a mediator, someone who can understand both worlds and help to bring them a little closer together. This can be and often is, the role of woman, for women, more easily than men, can stand with one foot in either world, and can ease the child's heartbreaking predicament.

But not only the child's for it is man's predicament as well. Woman as mediator can restore to him a world he has lost, a world that he needs if he is not to become as mechanical as the machines of his own invention, and as dessicated as the synthetic foods with which he is vainly trying to nourish himself.

It is, as I have said before in an earlier chapter, to Neumann, more than to anyone else, that we owe the realization that the consciousness which has been so hardly won by man over the centuries, liberating his mind from the primal unity of all things, is not the only kind of consciousness. There is also a more diffuse awareness which is yet far removed from a state of unconscious mist, and cannot be called *un*consciousness. Neumann calls this 'matriarchal consciousness' as distinct from the patriarchal consciousness of man's world.

I should like to quote from Neumann's Essay 'On the Moon and Matriarchal Consciousness':

> For matriarchal consciousness, understanding is not an act of the intellect, functioning as an organ for swift registration, development and organization; rather it has the meaning of a 'conception'. Whatever has to be understood must first 'enter' matriarchal consciousness in the full, sexual, symbolic meaning of a fructification. This means that the conceiving and understanding have brought about a personality change. The new content has stirred the whole being, whereas in patriarchal consciousness it would too often only have been filed in one

intellectual pigeon-hole or another. Just as a patriarchal consciousness finds it difficult to realize fully, and not merely meet with 'superb' understanding, so a matriarchal consciousness finds it difficult to understand without first 'realizing' and here to realize means to 'bear' to bring to birth: it means submitting to a mutual relation and interaction like that of the mother and embryo in pregnancy.

The comparative passivity of matriarchal consciousness is not due to any incapacity for action, but rather to an awareness of subjection to a process in which it can 'do' nothing, but can only 'let happen'. In all decisive life situations, the feminine, in a far greater degree than the nothing-but-masculine, is subjected to the numinous elements in nature or still better, has them 'brought home' to it. Therefore, its relation to nature and to God is more familiar and intimate, and its tie to an anonymous Transpersonal allegiance forms earlier and goes deeper than its personal tie to a man.[2]

You will have noticed that Neumann speaks of this feminine matriarchal consciousness as 'it'. He is indeed most emphatic that this type of consciousness, which I prefer to call diffuse awareness, can also be found in men. It is not a question of sex at all, but rather of a masculine or feminine attitude of mind, the possibilities of both being latent in every individual. Artists and poets of necessity have both.

None the less, woman tends to be more naturally guided by an inborn diffuse awareness than is man, and although she is seldom able to formulate the things of which she is aware, her very presence in a close relationship with a man will open the door, as it were, to the wealth of the collective unconscious in the man himself. So he also, in contact with his own diffuse awareness, finds the unity of all growing things.

I cannot stress too strongly that matriarchal consciousness or diffuse awareness is *not* identical with the formless chaos of the unconscious. It is emphatically *not* *un*consciousness. Its difference in quality from masculine focused consciousness with which we are all familiar, lies in its whole unbroken state which defies scientific analysis and logical deduction, and is therefore not possible to formulate in clear unambiguous terms.

2 *Spring*, 1954, Analytical Psychology Club of New York.

Woman's supreme role as mediator is here: between a man's ⌉
clear-cut intellect, and the awareness of wisdom and wholeness |
lying latent within himself.                                    ⌋

How woman achieves this mediation is a mystery. She certainly
will not succeed by attempting to explain. At best her words will
only bemuse. At worst they will sound ridiculous. Inability to
formulate the unformulatable is a hurdle she cannot jump. But
instinct has its own unerring ways. The seed sprouts in the dark
and ideas are germinated in the silence:

> When Eve uncovers on the salt sea bed a pearl,
> She does not claim her ownership
> Nor break it up to find the speck of sand within,
> Spoiling its opaque loveliness,
> But softly lets it fall in man's quiescent mind
> To save it from forgetfulness;
> And when one day it comes to light unsought,
> She marvels at the pearly iridescence of his thought.

Whether or not a woman knows that this is what she does, that
it was she who brought the pearl up from the depths of the unconscious, will depend upon the quality of her own *focused* consciousness. It takes a high degree of focused consciousness in a
woman for her to be able to observe what she is in fact doing
instinctively.

But please notice that Eve in the poem has not opened the door
to chaos, nor has she handed her man the bare ingredients of a
grain of sand and an oyster shell.

The pearl has been created, rounded and perfected. She did not ⌉
create it, but it was she who found it because it is she who is at |
home in the sea of the unconscious and can dive more easily      |
without being drowned. She brings up this symbol of wholeness,   |
unbroken and still opaque. Such pearls are her jewels of aware-  |
ness, her values which are utterly destroyed by man's dissection. A ⌋
dissected pearl has ceased to be.

Now do all women behave like this? I suspect some of my
readers will shake their heads with lack of recognition. Some will
be angry at the very idea. No, I am convinced that only a particular kind of woman plays this role of mediator to man of the
mysteries of his own psyche.

It was Toni Wolff who made a study of personality types in

women.[3] She was one of Dr. Jung's first and most important
collaborators, both in confronting the mysteries, beauty and
terror of the collective unconscious, and also as a brilliant
analyst.

During many years of analysis of all kinds of men and women
she observed that, quite apart from Jung's four psychological
functions of Thinking, Feeling, Intuition and Sensation, woman
can also be characterized by one or more of four distinct types of
personality. She emphasized that the younger generation tends to
combine at least two of these main types in contrast to older generations who seem more often to have been limited to one. And she
contended that the process of individuation in woman demands a
gradual assimilation of all four characteristic attitudes.

She calls these four basic feminine types, maternal, hetaira,
amazon and mediumistic and describes their respective relationship to man.

The maternal type is the most obvious, but I find it illuminating
that in her view this type not only cherishes all that is young and
tender and growing, but relates to the man principally as father to
her children. One can, I think, see this also in the intellectual
realm where a wife looks to the husband as the source of her ideas,
and readily accepts his notions on politics, religion or whatever it
may be, with the same blind wholehearted acceptance with which
she accepts his child. The 'mothering' which tends to become
smothering and which we so deprecatingly attribute to mothers is,
if I understand right, the negative side of the maternal which
cherishes where cherishing is no longer needed, and more likely
to arise from the unconscious in women who are actually not
mother-types.

There is a good parallel here to the functions. Bad thinking is
not the sin of thinking types. Nor is bad possessive mothering likely
to be the sin of real differentiated mother types. The compulsive
mothers are those whose maternal instinct comes rushing up from
the *un*conscious in a most *un*differentiated way. It is then that the
mother archetype takes charge and the woman feels like killing
anyone who touches or criticizes her offspring, and is quite unable
to distinguish between mothering and smothering.

It seems doubtful whether the maternal type as such acts as
mediator between a man and his unconscious though she may

[3] Toni Wolff, *Structural Forms of the Feminine Psyche*, Zürich, Students
Association, C. G. Jung Institute, 1956.

mediate between father and children. She does however care for and protect whatever is new and growing in the man, if it enhances his position or influence in *outer* life, as such things are important in his role of husband and father to the children.

On the other hand any aspect of his personal development which is outside the family boundary, or does not accrue to the family's benefit, is frowned upon as a dangerous menace to the family's welfare. The poor man's danger from a wife who is such an extreme maternal type is that he feels spiritually imprisoned, and only valued as a financial provider or a useful piece of furniture.

The extreme opposite and furthest away from the maternal type is, according to Miss Wolff, the hetaira or companion. This type relates to man for his own sake, not as father to her children. She can be a companion on any level, intellectually, spiritually or sexually or all three at once, but not necessarily all three. She may in extreme cases be a 'femme inspiratrice'. One frequently meets her in marriages where the children are only of secondary importance. And outside marriage she constantly fills the gap which a maternally oriented wife may leave in a husband's psyche, giving him value in himself, not only as husband and father.

To the hetaira the personal relationship with the man is all important. It is the only thing in life which matters. Everything else can be swept aside as irrelevant. She does indeed give value to the man but she also reflects his personal anima, with all its inspiration and its flattery, to such a degree that she may lapse into the role of seductress. If so, she may lure him away from his real destiny, or the practical necessities of outer life, in favour of some illusory anima ambition, and so ultimately ruin him.

It is of the utmost importance that a woman should know her hetaira potentialities both in their positive and dangerous aspects, for if they are repressed she may turn her sons into secret lovers and her daughters into close girl friends thus hampering their ability to make their own relationships.

Though readily carrying a man's anima it is to his *personal* unconscious that the hetaira type relates and so it is his personal unconscious which she can be said to mediate to him.

The hetaira is not an easy role for a woman to play as it does not fit into accepted patterns of society. Nor do the women of this type always realize that they have a definite role to play; so they continually try to change their status of mistress to that of wife,

mistakenly believing that marriage is the inevitable desired goal.
To quote once more from Toni Wolff:

> Everything in life must be learned, also human relationship;
> and it is therefore only natural that the hetaira cannot begin
> with it on the more differentiated levels. But once she has
> learned it, she will carefully observe the laws of individual re-
> lationship, she will notice what belongs to it and what not, and
> she will if necessary know when a relationship has become
> fulfilled and complete.

The hetaira woman who breaks other people's marriages in
order to become the wife herself has not yet learned what belongs
to her particular form of relationship.

The third type, the amazon, is one we are seeing more and more
frequently today. She is independent and self-contained. She is
primarily concerned with her own achievement. She claims
equality with men. Although she may have love affairs or even
marry and have children she is not dependent on the man for
fulfilment, as are both the maternal and hetaira types. She meets
man on a conscious level and in no way acts as mediator for him.
She frequently lives her love life like a man, sometimes even mis-
using her relationships to further her own career.

The suffragette was of course the unadulterated amazon whose
emergence filled men with horror. But today she has ceased to be
the hard masculinized woman of yesterday and, having found her
own level, no longer behaves as a menacing rival to man. Consciously he accepts her as a comrade, a pleasant work mate and a
worthwhile challenge which stirs his own endeavours. None the
less, I am pretty sure that in the unconscious of men, the appearance of the amazon is still both feared and hated. I can find
no other explanation for the persistence of the inner voice in every
woman I have ever met which dins into her ears the words, 'You
are no good.' I believe this is her negative animus picking up
man's collective unconscious fear of woman's rivalry, and his
passionate desire to keep her in her place. If men could become
more conscious of their inner disdain, women might become less
aggressive in self-defence against this insidious unconscious cor-
rosion.

The relationship of the amazon type to man is like that of
brother and sister. They understand one another, participate in

similar activities and act as mutual challengers and rivals. There seems no place here for the amazon type to play a mediator role.

Toni Wolff's fourth personality type is what she calls the mediumistic woman and here we have par excellence the woman whose principal role is that of mediator.

She is permeated by the unconscious of another person and makes it visible by living it. She may pick up what is going on beneath the surface of the group or society in which she lives, and voice it. I have known women who were working in a group to dream dreams which seemed unmistakably to be messages to the group as a whole. She may become permeated by a religious creed and put herself at its service. She may express in her own person the spirit of an epoch. Joan of Arc was such a one. Her voices from the collective unconscious speaking to her with the lips of saints, impelled her to live in her own person, and almost to bring into being, the spirit of nationhood which was trying to emerge in France. To quote Toni Wolff, 'The mediumistic type is rather like a passive vessel for contents which lie outside it, and which are either being simply lived or else are being formed.' In this sense she is immensely valuable in giving shape to what is still invisible. Women like Florence Nightingale or Elizabeth Fry were instrumental in bring to consciousness a humanitarian spirit which had been lying latent. Toni Wolff suggests that women writers sometimes have a flair for mediating to their own time some wholly other epoch. Mary Renault is surely one of these. *The King Must Die* and other novels by her seem quite miraculously evocative of the spirit of Ancient Greece.

On a more personal level I know one woman who dreamed a whole series of dreams pertaining not only to the man with whom she was in intimate contact but to his whole family. When she recounted them they were so dramatically relevant to his family situation that the man's attitude was changed and he was enabled to undertake a difficult task with his father which, before he was told the dreams, would have seemed utterly impossible.

I know other women who seem able to help men to die as their time approaches. These women may be aware that they do this. Sometimes the man in question also knows that the woman is fulfilling this strange role for him. But it is not always necessary to have an intimate relationship for such a thing to happen, and the emergence of such a mediator role may be as complete a surprise to the woman as to the man. I have met this in my own experience.

On one occasion I visited a man in hospital whom I did not know at all well, but who was a member of a society to which I belonged and with whom I had always felt some affinity. I visited him again when he was sent home to his wife to die. To my surprise he told me intimate things of his life which he had never before mentioned to anyone. I said almost nothing but when I rose to leave I kissed him lightly on the forehead. To my bewilderment he burst into tears. Without knowing at all what I was doing I had freed him from the dry prison of his intellect in which he had been immured and put him in touch with his own unconscious feeling, with its promise for the future. Next day his wife told me I was the only person he wanted to see. I sat by his bed and listened to his delirium. But it was no longer guilt-ridden. He had already embarked on a journey. He died that night.

Such a mediatory role was entirely unconscious and unforeseen. But I have known other women who appear to realize what they are doing. One of these was the wife of a modern high-ranking scientist, newly working in one of the old universities, and finding it difficult to adapt. She told me one day that she was haunted by a male figure in black medieval clothes who appeared every night in her dreams: *He wore a high pointed hat from the apex of which poured a cascade of fine black lace falling to the ground. Black lace covered his face and it was her business to encircle with small white feathers the point of his hat from where the black lace fell. He held in one hand a money box raised to the level of his head.*

As she woke each morning she clearly saw him standing by the bed. She was used to dreams but the insistence of this figure troubled her. I could not tell from what she told me whether he was a part of her psyche, which she needed to contact, or if she was picking up some unknown figure in the unconscious of her husband of which he was unaware. I suggested she should draw him. She did so and showed the picture to her husband. He had learned to respect her imagery. He looked carefully at the drawing. 'Yes,' he said, 'that belongs to me.' The dreams and the hallucination ceased. She had been the means of giving her husband an image from the collective psyche which concerned him and which he had needed to contact before he could feel at home in the medieval setting in which he actually found himself.

The mediumistic woman is, as Toni Wolff makes clear, not easy to discover, as she seldom appears in public and is not publicly recognized as having a definite role to play; yet it is she more than

mother, hetaira or amazon who renders the unique service to man
of mediating to him the contents of the collective unconscious. She
is also less visible than other types because today a woman is
seldom only mediumistic. She may also be a hetaira or a mother
type and then it may appear that it is the wife and mother who is
playing the mediating role, or perhaps a lover or woman friend.
So considerable confusion reigns and it is popularly believed that,
with the exception of the amazon, women as women tend to be
mediators. Even the amazon is seldom nothing but amazon. She
may combine in outer life maternal functions or be the gentlest,
most feminine mistress. Her amazon personality will only show in
her inability to commit herself to any dependent physical or
spiritual relationship to the man. But the amazon, whether coup-
led with mother or hetaira, is still unlikely to be mediumistic, for
medium and amazon are extreme opposite types, as are hetaira
and mother.

The mediumistic woman is elusive also because she has greater
difficulty than the other types of knowing who she really is. All
personality types, even the amazon are related in some way to the
masculine psyche since it is of the essence of the feminine to be
related to the masculine. But the mediumistic woman is always in
danger of losing her own ego in the personality of the man she
loves, or the group which claims her interest. She really does not
know if it is her own interest or feeling she is expressing or that of
the other.

I met one remarkable case of this seeming loss of identity in a
mediumistic woman who realized that in the absence of her husband or her son she felt completely vague, unfocused and at a loss.
She went to an analyst in the hope that he might help, but was
shattered by the following dream: *She visited her analyst and
looked into the mirror he held up for her, but to her horror there
was no reflection.* This dream convinced her, as nothing else could
have done, of her paramount need to learn to exist in her own
right and not merely as a mediator for other people. That she had
not understood how to achieve this was evidenced by another
dream two years later: *A voice said to her: 'Don't try to have a
reflection. Break the mirror.'*

Indeed it is vitally important for a woman who is to handle
images from the collective unconscious to have a strong ego, if she
is not to get lost in its mazes and cause confusion to herself and
those around her. She must be able to know the difference between

the world of images and the world of everyday if she is to stand in the middle and mediate one to the other. So the task of acquiring ego consciousness, or patriarchal consciousness as Neumann would call it, is more difficult for the mediumistic woman than for the other personality types, but even more imperative.

Moreover, it is not enough today for any woman to be limited to one personality type any more than it is enough for a man to have only one psychological function at his disposal. The inner process which demands wholeness is as vividly at work in women as in men. When stuck in one personality type something forces a woman to develop a second, then a third and finally a fourth.

I should not like to give the impression that the mediumistic woman, mediator as she is, is wholly positive for man. She not only suffers more than most women from ego uncertainty which makes relationships difficult, but she can also be extremely dangerous. She may see too far and too deeply into the unconscious to be comfortable for those around her. As the mother of a family she may work havoc. She is apt to know what is happening before it has become visible in outer life and she is seldom wise enough to keep her knowledge to herself. Even if she does not voice her findings, she conveys them whether she means to do so or not.

This may be bearable in her relationship to a man but it can be disastrous for her children. The supreme need of growing youth is ability to experience for themselves, free from prying eyes, perhaps even from their own. Growth takes place in the dark places of the psyche. The unknown flower which will emerge is the delight of discovery. The mediumistic mother may, without any effort on her part, already know the type and colour of the flower still bedded tightly in its bud, for, in the unconscious, time has no meaning and all things are already known. If she mediates her knowledge to those around her, though she speaks no word, she will have robbed her young of the fullness of their own experience.

I know one mother who was constantly having dreams warning of this danger. She had considerable psychological insight and constantly feared that she was being over-protective to her children. But the dreams pointed to a wholly other danger: *In one dream there was a great mastiff guarding the door of her house. Little chicks were climbing all over him without his moving a muscle or showing any desire to pounce on them, or crush them with a paw.*

*A voice said, 'Your dog will do your chicks no harm. Look in the backyard for the marauder.' And there she saw an owl feeding with the hens, no one noticing that he is the enemy of little birds and eggs.*

The dreamer digested this as best she could but some years later had another far more frightening dream: *She saw an immense hollow tree, an entrance near the base. Outside the entrance was again an image of small animals, but this time they were kittens lying peacefully in a kind of nest.*

*She peered inside the hollow tree and saw to her surprise all sorts of animals big and little. As she looked a lioness strolled out and walked among her own children outside the tree. The lioness moved among them easily without the shadow of a menace and it was clear that the children neither did nor had need to fear her. Then the dreamer looked higher within the hollow trunk and at the top of it she saw fiery luminous snakes reach out from the walls of the tree, their heads meeting together in the centre. It was the light they emitted which made the contents of the whole tree visible. Alarmed at their dangerous proximity to the children she stepped back. 'That tree must be smoked out immediately,' she said.*

Whether she was right that the tree should be smoked out seems highly doubtful. These fiery snakes, which being at the top of the tree presumably stand for spiritual insight, do appear to be shown as the dangerous element in contrast to the harmless lioness. To smoke them out would, for the woman, have been to lapse into a state of semi-consciousness and forego the fruits of years of analysis. The dream was perhaps telling her to close the door of the tree so that the snakes could neither emerge, nor the children wander inside inadvertently.

Although woman's role as mediator lies in her capacity to mediate the unconscious to man, not all women do this. The hetaira type will reflect for him the attitudes of his personal anima, but in order to mediate the contents of the collective unconscious to him, a woman needs to have an ingredient of the medium type in her make-up.

Moreover if she is to be a good mediator and not just open the door to that very chaos man has left behind him, woman needs to have, along with her own diffuse feminine awareness, enough masculine ego consciousness to be able to discriminate between these two forms of consciousness. She needs to know which world she is in at any given moment, never confusing one with the other. She needs to know that one world cannot be expressed in the language of the other, but that the more she herself is aware of who she is and where she stands the more likely will she be to hand man, not the chaos of the collective unconscious, but pearls, opaque yet formed, from the realm of diffuse awareness.

*Editor's note:* This chapter has been concerned with a woman's roles in her relationship with men. But the author wanted to add a further section about relationships between women, which she felt to be of great importance, and different in kind.

She was pondering these additional pages during the last days of her life, but did not write her thoughts down.

# V

# The Animus—Friend or Foe?

IN MY EARLIER chapters I have tried to distinguish between the feminine and masculine way of functioning within the same person whether man or woman and, following Jung, I have referred to the masculine in a woman as the animus. The following is an attempt to clarify what is meant by this obscure term.

Most men recognize that their women folk are not always their feminine selves but constantly behave or talk more as didactic men do, or get emotional about some matter which does not call for emotion, all of which they find irritating and disconcerting. Occasionally the woman notices it herself. It is as though a man suddenly obtruded into a woman's psyche from time to time and made remarks on his own. Sometimes he even seems to be in total possession, overshadowing the woman herself until she can hardly be seen. This masculine appearance in a woman's psyche we call the animus, and as he is most noticeable when he is being objectionable he has earned a bad name for himself.

My purpose is to show that the animus, who is indeed like a woman's male partner, is not only irritating and destructive but is of the utmost value, and is essential for any creativeness on her part.

The first thing to stress is the collective nature of this figure. Like the anima of a man he is the personification of a function which belongs in the psyche of all women and is not a personal idiosyncrasy.

To be possessed by the animus may be a misfortune but it is not a personal disgrace. Unfortunately, our habit of talking about Mrs. Smith's animus or Mr. Brown's anima causes confusion, making one forget that the personal guise worn by these images is only a cloak covering the eternal collective figures which animate them.

Where emotions are rising quite unnecessarily in any discussion and people are getting hot under the collar, it is an enormous help if we can learn to stop saying, as we point an accusing finger, 'You said so-and-so,' which only makes it worse, and instead call a halt and say, 'Oh damn! the devil has got into this, we shall have to start afresh.' Not your devil, nor my devil, but *the* devil.

The following remarks are based entirely on personal experience, my own and that of the women who have come my way. I do not want to draw conclusions, but to throw out a few ideas which have occurred to me for further study, and to hand over to you a few practical tips which I have found useful in dealing with this difficult partner of ours.

When I speak of woman I mean *basic woman* — which of course none of us are. Similarly, I am using the word man to mean basic male, which no actual man is either.

Some years ago (I was already working as a psychotherapist) I had the following dream: '*I was walking peacefully along a country lane when I met a band of men, a dozen or so, going in the opposite direction, accompanied by a sort of wireless apparatus. I knew in the dream that, though they looked harmless enough, they were a menace to me, and I felt extremely frightened. But I was told that I could pass them in safety if I saluted each one in turn, saying the words,* 'palabra de honor'. *This is Spanish for* 'word of honour', *but in Spain honour is more sacrosanct than here. Honour is the value for which one would give one's very life. So* 'palabra de honor' *is the most sincere and dramatic password a Spaniard could devise.* (I must explain that my husband was a Spaniard and that I lived in Spain for many years, but the stress on honour in the dream will also tell you that I personally speak from the opposite standpoint of extreme femininity. What follows may not fit other types of women.) *This ritual I solemnly carried out, saluting each man in turn and repeating to each the password,* 'palabra de honor'.

There was a great deal more to the dream but I want to use this as my opening scene, for I have come back to it again and again during the succeeding years, each time with a little more understanding that this is the key, the magic password which will turn the animus from foe to friend.

First of all note that there are a number of men and each one in turn has to be placated. We know that the animus often appears as a group, a committee, a jury, etc. This group of men in my dream, however, was not a homogeneous group which could be dealt with as a whole. Each man had to be saluted separately. I believe this to be fundamental. In trying to contact the animus we tend to think of him as one person, although we know he has a multitude of shapes. He can appear as an old man or as a little boy, a learned scholar or an aviator, a god or a devil, a romantic lover or the prosaic figure who styles himself one's husband.

To any of these we can talk, but we can no more talk to the animus with a capital A than we can talk to man with a capital M. Nor is it enough to remember that the animus is dual, both positive and negative. For instance, if an evil-looking man appears at my door in a dream it is no use my recalling that though this may be a dark side of the animus he also has a light aspect, because then I am powerless to deal with him. How can I grapple with a robber if I am thinking 'After all, if only I could see his other side he might by my guardian angel.' This paralyses one from a true reaction. I believe one needs to act in as single-minded a way to each facet of the animus as one would to a real man. I should not in actual life wait to be robbed or raped. I should ask an intruder what he wanted. If I did not like his answer I should request him to go away. I should be quite indifferent to this man's possible good intentions. One reacts directly to the aspect of man which presents itself. So also to the animus.

Now, if only we can succeed in splitting the animus up into distinct and separate persons we can deal with him. Then I can kneel and ask a blessing of the priest, befriend the feeble-minded boy, face firmly, but with due respect, the devil and order the mealy-mouthed sycophant out of my house. But woe betide me if I lump them all together, call it the animus, and try to deal with that.

I know one woman who has a great deal of active imagination and talks to some twenty different aspects of her animus under different names. She will say: 'I had a refreshing talk with Jim, the cowboy, yesterday,' or 'My learned friend Andrew told me so-and-so.' But one day, in a rash, adventurous moment, she collected them all together in one room, and was surprised to find her knees shaking with terror at the assembled power she had conjured up. She dealt with the situation by very humbly addressing her grandfather, who was one of the company, and beseeching his help and protection.

Note, please, that every aspect of the animus is personified separately and, if one is to have a true relationship with the whole, each of these separate persons must be dealt with separately, in all sincerity of feeling, from the depth of one's being. There can be no half measures, no false sentiments, no rationalized devaluation of one's feeling towards any one of them. There must be no mere lip service to the priest, no cringing to the bully, no idle blustering to the devil:

> To thine own self be true,
> And it must follow, as the night the day,
> Thou canst not then be false to any man.

This is as valid for a woman's relationship to her animus as to any human being. *Palabra de honor*. Utter sincerity is the password. My life depends on my acceptance of this most masculine conception, honour.

To be sincere with one's own animus! That is the key to this relationship as to every other. How simple, and how difficult! For to be sincere to one's own true feelings, to stand for one's own inner knowledge, demands that one should know what one's feelings are and what one's inner knowledge is. To see clearly enough to know something quite definitely, so solidly that one can express it and say 'This is my truth, here I take my stand,' one needs the help of the animus himself.

I personally like to think of my helpful animus as a torch-bearer: the figure of a man holding aloft his torch to light my way, throwing its beams into dark corners and penetrating the mists which shield the world of half-hidden mystery where, as a woman, I am so very much at home.

In a woman's world of shadows and cosmic truths he makes a pool of light as a focus for her eyes, and as she looks she may say, 'Ah yes, that's what I mean,' or 'Oh no, that's not my truth at all.' It is with the help of this torch also that she learns to give form to her ideas. He throws light on the jumble of words hovering beneath the surface of her mind so that she can choose the ones she wants, separates light into the colours of the rainbow for her selection, enables her to see the parts of which her whole is made, to discriminate between this and that. In a word, he enables her to focus.

To me it seems that the power to focus is the essential quality which makes man the creative creature that he is. Sparkling ideas or images of incredible loveliness may float through the mind of almost anyone; float through and out again, unused, unavailing and unhoused. But he who has the ability to focus, see and hold the idea as it emerges, can create something with it. He can build a temple or a philosophy. He can build an atom bomb.

Ability to focus is not the same as ability to think, although a strange confusion seems to have arisen here in many women's minds. I have constantly heard the thinking function of a woman equated with animus, but this is a misunderstanding. Thinking is a function, a fundamental way of approaching life like any other function.

The ability to focus applies irrespective of function. Focusing is not the same as thought, though, certainly, there can be no creative thinking without the power to focus. But neither can feeling be creative without the power to hold the nameless joy or pain, and out of it give birth. Intuitions, glinting with iridescent colours, are of no more value than a pest of flies buzzing round one's head, if there is no power to focus on one of them and give it life. Sensation, reality, can be a prison if there is no power to focus on some aspect of it and change its shape.

The power to focus is man's greatest gift but not man's prerogative; the animus plays this role for a woman. He is the same in kind as the spirit which imbues man and makes him a creative being, but different in quality for, dwelling in the unconscious as he does, woman contacts him indirectly, as it were. But there he is functioning more or less well whenever she focuses on anything in order to see what it really is, whenever she analyses, discriminates, selects, formulates, creates.

Please do not misunderstand me. By focusing I do not mean consciousness. Woman (remember I mean basic woman) has a consciousness of her own, a 'diffused awareness'. Everything is accepted, enjoyed or hated as a whole. She feels herself equally at one with the stars or a drop of dew, a rose or a blade of grass. She does not analyse them nor want to do anything about them. She is simply aware. For man, and again I refer to the extreme male, the scent of the rose is not enough. He must learn all he can about it, prune and graft the plant to obtain even better roses. No woman, as woman, does such things. They would not occur to her.

Yet woman is not just earth. To be told, as she often is told by psychologists, that man represents the spirit and she the earth, is one of those disconcerting things a woman tries hard to believe, knowing all the time that they are not true; knowing that the pattern provided does not fit, however hard she tries to squeeze herself into it. She is not merely blind nature and life force. She has a spiritual awareness of her own which has little to do with the masculine culture in which we live, and nothing to do with philosophy and cosmologies. If she has succeeded — and not all women succeed — in holding on to her true feminine soul in spite of the weight on her shoulders of the masculine education she is asked to carry, she will dimly recognize her own direct spiritual awareness, which she is nonetheless wholly unable to express and almost unable even to admit. Her innermost feminine soul is as dumb and as shy as is any man's anima. But her awareness is there, diffuse and all-pervading. She can walk in the dark and place her feet as delicately as a cat without any light from her animus's torch.

It is only when she needs a focused kind of consciousness that the help of the animus is needed, and today she needs this most of the time. And there he is, always at hand, with his torch ready lit. The trouble is that he does not always shine it on the right things. At the slightest beckon of her finger he appears, throws his light in answer to her question on what seems to be the formula she seeks, and out she comes with a slogan, correct enough probably as a general truth, or in its rightful context, but just irrelevant to the matter in hand, or the particular case. When he is wide of the mark he is not so dangerous because his bad aim is apparent. Often, however, he is only a hair's breadth away from the truth and then sounds so plausible that, unperceived, in a few minutes the woman, and not infrequently her hearers, have been subtly led far astray from the matter in hand. Friend has turned foe.

This sudden insidious turn of face is a phenomenon we all know only too well. It may happen in a discussion between two people and it inevitably leads to irritation. But it also happens when a woman is talking to herself, the animus being one of the persons taking part in the conversation. Then, indeed, he becomes her most deadly foe for, without seeing where or how, she is flung or, worse, gently led right out of her own path into a morass of conventional ideas where she may flounder helplessly for weeks or months until she suddenly realizes who is at the bottom of the trouble. If only she can catch him at it she is saved. She can then face her adversary and, with a stamp of the foot, order him to get out of her way. Instantaneously, she will find herself on safe ground, again on her own pathway, the fog cleared — until next time. (Let it be a real stamp of the foot and the command 'get out' given in a loud voice; unless she is a woman used to commanding in real life, in which case she may need to learn the opposite technique of an appeal for help or a bewitching smile.)

Now why does this occur? It almost looks like deliberate evil intent on the part of the animus. It is certainly this behaviour which gives him such a bad name and enables us to hurl the word 'animus-y' at our neighbour with such opprobrium. But is it really his fault? And is it really his particular delight to be so destructive?

Barbara Hannah,[1] in a paper on the animus, quoted his answer to this question. He told her that he understood nothing of her world, but that he could not bear a vacuum, so he always slipped in when a vacuum occurred. He told her that he needed to know about our world as much as we needed to know about his, and that it is a woman's business to enlighten him. In my own talks with the animus on this point he has expressed a similar idea, using the particular imagery in which he has shown himself to me. He has explained that he, the torchbearer, is an autonomous spirit whose sole concern is shedding light, focused light, light for its own sake. He has no feelings towards us, neither good nor ill, he has no feelings of any kind. Feeling is a human prerogative. He has no interest in us one way or another except, and this is vitally important, that he needs us for his very existence, for it is only in the human mind that he can dwell. He needs a human being to see the light he sheds. But shed his focusing light he must. To me, this is who he is.

In this sense, and in this sense only, has he any concern in our becoming conscious, for the more conscious we are the more we use his torch; and the more he is an essential part of us, a comrade and a partner, the nearer we approach that impossible goal of individuation.

So, it would appear that he sheds his light on whatever he thinks we will look at. If we appeal to him as a friend and ask him to throw his light on different aspects of the problem in hand he will surely do so. If our aim is the pursuit of some particular study he will readily put his torch at our disposal. Intellectual and professional women have all gained his friendship, sometimes, it is true, handing over the rein to him and allowing him to run their lives, carry through their careers or write their books for them. In these cases the animus may or may not be the dominant partner in the concern, but he is being creative. A woman who, with his aid,

[1] Analyst and lecturer of the C. G. Jung Institute, Zürich.

has made herself a student on, say, medieval churches or the treat-
ment of cancer, no matter what, even though it be to the exclusion
of a domestic life, may be called an animus woman, but will
probably not be 'animus-y', for her animus is purposefully used
and directed.

It is the woman who is not using the animus creatively who is at
his mercy for he *must* throw his light somewhere. So he attracts
her attention by throwing his light on one formula or slogan after
another quite regardless of their exact relevance. She falls into the
trap and accepts what he shows her as gospel truth.

A metallic note in a woman's voice or some physical rigidity will
announce his presence; it may be a stiffening of the shoulders; a
slight twist of the lips or rigidity of the whole body. Words are
powerless to remove him. Only action can do so — an affectionate
gesture, a playful shake or even a cup of tea!

*Irrelevance* is, I believe, the unmistakable hallmark of a negative animus statement. If looked at in isolation, animus generalizations are mostly sound remarks in themselves, for they are the
fruit of experience garnered through the ages and they express the
moral code of the place and time in history in which we live. But
they may happen to be irrelevant to the living moment.

So we come to this: the animus is a woman's greatest friend
when he shines his light on what is relevant, and turns foe the
moment he lapses into irrelevance. A woman once dreamed that
she saw four people spitting into the open mouth of a frog who in
his turn croaked forth their spittle. On painting the dream, she
realized that three of the spitters were the three analysts with
whom she had worked at different times and the fourth was her
own helpful animus. Everything that these four had said to her of
meaning and significance at one time or another had been swallowed by this cold-blooded, amphibious creature, who later dis-
gorged their remarks, out of their context, at inappropriate
moments, causing her infinite distress. This frog is a perfect
example of an animus figure whose destructiveness was solely
due to the irrelevance of his croaking.

The reader may have noticed that I have myself fallen into the
unhelpful way of talking of the animus as if he were one and
undivided. I have deliberately left this lapse as an illustration of
how easily this mistake can be made. When in moments of forget-
fulness I accuse the helpful animus of going round and round me
in sickening circles, he pulls me up at once. He says that was not he

but his fool of a brother, to whom he hands his torch when I won't look at what he is trying to show me.

How can a woman detect the difference? For such discrimination needs the help of the animus himself, the very fellow who appears to be causing the trouble. There is only one way that I know of grappling with this difficulty. The woman must use every endeavour to give him all the data she can find. Animus opinions are based on insufficient knowledge of facts: 'the majority is always right,' 'where there is a will there is a way,' 'psychology is not to be trusted,' or any other half truth. So also, in an inner dialogue, what the animus tells her will be a valueless generalization unless she gives him all the facts; above all, the facts of her feelings, their intensity, their object.

How often a woman will listen to her animus telling her that her children should be pushed out of the nest or, if he shifts his torch a little, that a home should be provided for them until they are ready to fly. Either might be wrong in a particular case. How often he will tell her that her love affair is a shallow business, bound to end soon because love affairs always do: or that she must not trust the man because men are always fickle; and she omits, simply omits, to tell the animus the depth of her own feeling, the nature of the particular man or the significance of the affair. Having no feelings himself, he does not know these relevant facts, and she, as likely as not, is too shy, too lacking in confidence, even of her own image of the animus and above all too unaware of his power and his prevalence, to tell him the truth.

Yet her honesty would have got her past a menacing animus in safety; it would even have turned the foe to friend, for he is as willing to throw his light upon what is relevant for her to see, as to destroy her by showing her inappropriate generalities. The password is on her lips if she will but say: 'My feeling is this. These are the things which matter to me. Here I take my stand.'

But how seldom we do this. Today women have become so immersed in a masculine world of ideas and principles that they forget their own basic truth. For instance, any educated woman can understand the principles of freedom and democracy for which we fight our wars. With her trained masculine mind she may agree that wars are inevitable — nay, praiseworthy; but if she is true to the basic woman in herself she must never forget for one moment that the death of every single man slain by a machine for a principle is an outrage far greater than a murder committed in

F

anger; that torture and enslaving on the altar of ideology is to her the vilest of human crimes.

To a woman who is true to her basic self, *un*relatedness is the touchstone of abomination. She must never forget that *un*related sexual intercourse much as she may enjoy it, festers in her belly; and that spiritual and intellectual achievements which are destructive of life cause the air which she breathes to stink. These are the things she must remember and of which she must constantly tell the animus, if he is to guide her aright through the maze of a masculine culture whose walls are lined with precepts. It is only if he knows her truest feelings, feelings upon which she takes her irrevocable stand, that he can be relied upon to throw his light on what is relevant to *her*, relevant to the situation, relevant to the living moment.

Maurice Nicoll in *The New Man*[2] speaks of the different *levels* of meaning in Christ's parables and of how the disciples often accepted the shallow meaning instead of the deeper one. The Devil, says Nicoll, is the creature who mixes up the levels, and this seems to me a description par excellence of the animus at his most satanic.

Mixing of the levels is the most diabolical form of irrelevance. But if you can still bear to follow my imagery you will see that it is the same thing. The focusing torch of the animus is destructive whenever it fails to hit the mark exactly, whether it be beside the point, too high or too low.

Talking on different levels without being quite aware of the fact is, as I have described in the chapter on 'Meeting', one of the most common and disastrous causes of misunderstanding between a man and a woman.

Our need is to keep the balance between masculine focused consciousness and woman's diffuse awareness — or, if you prefer, between the creative spirit which uses man as its vehicle and the life force which uses woman. Both these great impersonal forces are equally ruthless. They meet in the human mind, and I believe it is the task of every individual man and woman to help humanize them both. It seems today as though we have lost this vital balance.

The so-called emancipation of woman has resulted in women invading what was hitherto man's world in every branch. In other words they are living the life of the animus. There would be nothing wrong in that if it were not that in going over to man's

2 Maurice Nicoll, *The New Man*, Stuart and Richards, London, 1968.

world, woman's essential values so often get thrown overboard. Even when biologically a woman is fulfilling her role, getting married and having a family, there is still a tendency for her life energy or libido to be elsewhere: sending her child to a crèche while she takes a job, reading a book while she is breast-feeding her baby.

Hovering over this now familiar situation I see an enormous menacing question mark: has woman's libido gone so far over to the masculine world of ideas and mechanics that the feminine passionate concern with life is actually denuded of the libido which it needs in order to hold the balance between the opposites? Is this imbalance perhaps one of the deep-rooted causes of the most devastating wars the world has ever known?

On the other hand, even among apparently domesticated women there are many today fighting to be allowed to live something other than the hitherto accepted biological pattern. Their masculine aspirations are sincere attempts to fulfil themselves. The battle for these women is a hard one for they do not know who they are nor on what to take their stand. A traditional inner voice still tells them that, not being career women, their only duty is to be wives and mothers, and this voice is picked up by the animus and shouted at them through a megaphone at every opportune and inopportune moment, or dropped like poison into their ears when they are relaxed.

Woe betide such a woman who falls into the hands of a psychologist who believes it is the feminine side which needs to be fostered. For then the animus voices are strengthened a hundredfold and the poor woman feels caught in a vicious circle. Every blow in self-defence is hurled back at her as unwarrantable animus aggression, and the familiar little imp who tells her she is no good grows fat and laughs and crows over her more than ever. In attacking the aggressive animus we actually feed this other animus figure who is a far greater menace to the woman herself. (I will return to this little imp presently.)

Her only way out of the impasse is to salute in all solemnity her most helpful animus and to tell him that on her word of honour she is not pining to have a baby and that her most sincere aspiration is creation in another field, intellectual, artistic, or maybe that most precious of all creations for a woman: conscious, human relationship. Then the taunting voices cease and the chains drop away. She can sigh with relief and accept herself as she really is: a human being with spiritual aspirations who, though born a woman, was not born to procreate. If she can accept this, then her energy is freed and she can develop along the lines of her own destiny.

Whether she makes a relationship to a real man or to her own creative animus she will have fulfilled her woman's need and lived her woman's role. Relationship with an actual man is of course the easiest way of learning to relate to her own creative animus; but merely the affirmation that she has to go her individual way and not the way of biology will turn her animus, hitherto her enemy because he knew no better, into her friend and ally, helping her to attain the very goal which before he slandered. You see, he does not care which way it is. Relationship, tenderness and cherishing are no concern of his. He is an archetype, with no human qualities whatever.

But note that it is not knowledge which the animus provides. If the knowledge needed is to be found in books, he enables a woman to gain it by throwing his light on the page so that she can read the words. Whether or not she understands the words she reads will depend upon her education and her power to think as well as on her ability to focus. This is a question of type, not of animus. If the knowledge to be gained is within, waiting to be drawn out from the storehouse of the collective unconscious, here also the role of the animus is, I believe, principally one of focusing and collecting.

If I am not mistaken it is through his anima that a man receives his inspirations. She is the fountain from which he drinks. She holds the treasures in her lap and offers them when he is ready to receive her gifts. But, having received them, it is his masculine, discriminating mind which gives form to the elusive riches she offers. She is the *femme inspiratrice*. It rests with him to mould the inspiration.

But the animus is not a woman's inspiration. He holds no treasures. Woman is vaguely aware of being herself in direct touch with the mysterious source, but her awareness is so diffuse that she can seldom even speak of it. She needs, passionately needs, the animus's torch to light up for her the things which she already innately knows, so that she can know she knows them. He brings no treasures, but he can throw the light of his torch on to one of the myriad jewels nestling darkly in her lap so that she can pick it up and, holding one glistening gem in the hollow of her hand, can say, 'Look what I have found.' Without his help she cannot braid her mermaid's hair, nor weave into a poem her wordless songs. Without his help she cannot catch the coloured fragrance of her world and show it clearly even to herself.

I have here a picture which I drew some years ago to illustrate what I have just been saying.

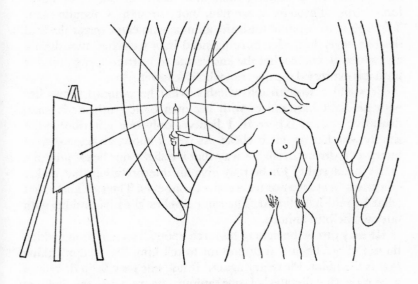

The huge figure behind is the Source. You may call her the Great Mother or you may call her the Nature Self which thrusts its children out into the everyday world to seek their own little ego-consciousness before they can find her again, at long last, as the Self of Becoming. But whatever you call her she is the Source from which the little girl, unlike the boy, is never separated. The woman standing between her giant knees is in direct intimate contact with her. The woman is drawing and in order to do so she uses the animus in the shape of her phallic pencil. He is the torch which throws light on her canvas, on herself and on the great figure behind; and note that by the aid of his light she can see that the Source is also winged, also a spiritual figure. The animus is the woman's measuring rod, her light and actually the pencil she uses, but her inspiration is gathered from her direct contact with the Source itself.

A woman today lives in perpetual conflict. She cannot slay the dragon of the unconscious without severing her own essential contact with it; without in fact destroying her feminine strength and becoming a mere pseudo-man. Her task is a peculiarly difficult one. She needs the focused consciousness her animus alone can give her, yet she must not forsake her woman's role of mediator to man. Through a woman, man finds his soul. She must never forget this. Through a woman, not through a pseudo-man. Through man, woman finds the animus who can *express* the soul she has never lost. Her burning need is to trust her own diffuse awareness, to *know* what she knows and to learn to speak of it, for until it is expressed she does not wholly know it.

How can a woman tell whether what her animus shows her with his light harmonizes with her own basic truth, or is some deceptive slogan? There is, I believe, only one criterion: quite simply whether or not it clicks. As we all know, an analyst may interpret a dream in such a way that we shake our heads and say, 'That is not right.' Or he may give an interpretation that makes our hearts beat faster or tears come to our eyes. Then we know that what he said has clicked. The same applies in conversations with our own helpful animus.

He may throw the light of his torch upon all sorts of things which do not click. Then it is important to tell him, 'No, I don't think that is the point. Please try again.' If not, one may be in danger of accepting the dictates of one animus figure with the help of another who likes to hear what he has heard before, or who tells us that we *ought* to accept whatever is told us by the unconscious. But if we are stirred, if we weep, there is no doubt that what the animus is telling us truly belongs, for a woman's tears accompany her deepest truth. An emotional response is usually a woman's surest guide to what belongs to her. But even when she discovers what belongs to her, she still has the greatest difficulty in telling her animus what she means, not only because she cannot focus enough to give form to her ideas, but because she does not seem to have adequate language at her disposal.

A woman uses the only language she has learned, yet in her own mind makes it fit her conception of the ideas, quite oblivious that her husband means something very different.

Two words that shine out in this connection are *Love* and *Spirit*.

I speak more of love in another setting but the word *Spirit* must be dealt with here for it is a great cause of confusion, both between actual men and women and between a woman and her animus.

To a woman, spirituality, or a life of the Spirit, implies relationship in its very essence: relationship to God in those intangible fleeting moments when she is aware of a presence, whether it be in the sudden impact of a white cherry tree in blossom, or the rhythmical furrows of a ploughed field; whether it be in a moment of unforgettable union with another human being or alone in the stillness of her own silence. Wherever it may happen there is for her always relationship. But the word 'spiritual' is not, I think, generally used in this sense. In the minds of many women the word Spirit evokes a memory of some direct experience very near to an awareness of the Holy Ghost.

If only she would voice her difficulty all would be well. But more often than not she is too bewildered by this difference in the use of words even to speak of her bewilderment. She neither tells her man of her failure to understand what he is saying, nor tells her own helpful animus and inner guide of her distress. If an analyst uses the expression 'spiritual animus' to convey the idea of something bad which is taking her away from life, then her bewilderment reaches its climax. That there is an animus who takes her away from life we all know very well. He may be the animus of collective ideas, of what is 'done'; he may be an intellectual recluse, a puritanical prig, or a pseudo-mystic. Any of these can seduce a woman away from life, but for the sake of mutual understanding let us not call him spiritual; for that word, to a woman, touches the highest that she knows and is imbued with a sacred relatedness which can never be destructive, for it is the giver of meaning to life.

Indeed, the expression 'spiritual animus' is, to a woman, a contradiction in terms. The animus is by his very nature an *in*human spirit and is therefore in his essence *un*related. Whereas to be spiritual is to her the very essence of relationship. It would be a help if the animus were only called spiritual when a woman has really succeeded in making a vivid relationship with him and he can be relied upon to co-operate as a friend.

If a woman will only be honest and stand her ground in a conversation with her own animus whenever there is something wrong, he will cease reiterating, parrot-wise, the same old saws. He may perhaps show her where she has not understood the meaning of what she has been told. He may even enable her to see, in a sudden flash from his illuminating torch, that the giving she had thought was love was little more than nature's flow of sap, the surging forth of life which uses her; and that to love, really to love, she needs the full co-operation of her partner, the animus, to direct her giving to the measure of the need. It is not love to choke one's children with more milk than they can swallow. Nor, if a man asks for a sip of water, is it love to drown him in a water-fall.

And in her turn she may make the animus understand — perhaps she may even make some man understand who had not known it before — that the essence to her of a spiritual life is one of relatedness.

I should like to say a little more about the animus that is woman's worst bugbear. He is the one who tells her she is no good. This voice is particularly dangerous because it only speaks to the woman herself and she is so cast down by it that, as likely as not, she dare not tell anyone about it and ask for help. In fact, it seldom occurs to her to do so. On the contrary, without knowing it, the analyst or anybody else, in any criticism, no matter how kindly made, is always in danger of actually feeding this de-structive little imp, more particularly if a woman's aggression is really expressing her powerlessness to get across what she means, her defence of the half-glimpsed treasures which she knows are there but for which she can find no words. Then anyone's attack upon the aggressive animus will so bolster up this demon who shouts or whispers, 'You see, I was right, you *are* no good,' that the woman can be almost crushed by it.

And yet even this little wretch can also become an asset if only one will face him and say, 'Why do you tell me I'm no good, when in fact I have done so and so and achieved such and such, have lived through this and that crisis without wavering?' Gradually one amasses one's good qualities and one's achievements until his 'You're no good' looks silly. In other words this poisonous little voice forces one in sheer self-defence to be conscious of who one really is. His poison, like many another poison, brings healing.

Once the animus has become a friend upon whom one can rely, I believe a still further achievement with him can be reached. I speak of this with much diffidence, for, although I have it on his own authority, it may not sound convincing. But I pass on his message to me, to take or leave as you will. *He can and should be changed.* That he does change is obvious enough when one recalls that the moral precepts he voices at any one time and place in history differ from the moral precepts of some other time and place.

But what of our individual responsibility to change him? I believe if only women will hold true to their values as women and constantly tell the animus: 'Here I take my stand,' to an infinitesimal degree they may change the words he utters, not only to themselves, but also to other women. If we will tell our helpful animus, and continually repeat, that to the basic woman in us the slaughter of our sons and the crippling or enslaving of life anywhere is monstrous and unforgivable, then we may do the inestimable service of helping to keep in balance the two ruthless forces between which we are impaled, crude nature and relentless mind.

Moreover, in any close man–woman relationship, if the woman takes her stand on her own deepest truth and feelings, she not only makes a relationship of sincerity to her own animus, but the man's attitude will, sometimes without any word or explanation, change too. One constantly sees this happen in marriage-problem cases when only the wife is having an analysis.

How does this come about? For one thing, when a woman ceases to project her own aspect of the negative animus on to her man, he becomes free to function unhampered by this incubus. But perhaps also, on a deeper level, when a woman turns the animus from foe to friend and keeps him faithfully informed of her deepest feelings, these may seep through the ground and fruitfully water the thoughts and ideas of man himself.

# VI

# *The Second Apple*[1]

WHEN ADAM ATE the apple offered him by Eve he was thrown out of Paradise. He had ceased to be an innocent follower of instinctive nature for he had stolen a fragment of God's creativeness. He had stolen the power to choose.

Man had gained the power to obey nature or defy her. Man had sinned. No animal can sin as it has no choice. It can only obey the laws of its being. Man alone can sin.

And ever since that unfortunate incident of the apple men have felt guilty, and have done their best to make women feel guilty too.

Still, in the twentieth century, after the birth of a baby, our Christian Churches demand that a woman shall be ritually 'cleansed' by the priest, implying that she has sinned. Yet if there is ever a moment in a woman's life when she does not feel sinful it is when she has given birth. If she is truly in touch with her *own* feelings I cannot conceive that anything will ever make her believe that the act which led to the conception of her child could possibly have been a sin.

The woman with a newborn baby by a man she loves is as nearly in tune with nature as she can ever be, and when we are in tune with nature we feel ourselves to be in a state of grace, not sin.

I believe the sense of sin surrounding the sexual act is not indigenous to feminine psychology, but has been superimposed upon her by man and fostered quite especially by the Church. All the nonsense talked about the sacredness of woman's virginity, 'more precious than life itself,' is, I believe, far more a relic of man's claim to ownership than anything else. On the contrary in my limited experience, deep in the unconscious of most women lurks a primitive desire to be raped. This does not square with a passion for virginity, though one can certainly say that a desire to be raped in

[1] The image of 'The Second Apple' was given to me by my daughter Jacinta Castillejo de Nadal.

the unconscious is to be expected where there is an overvaluation of virginity in the conscious mind. But 'virginity' used not to mean lack of sexual experience. The 'Virgin' Goddesses were those who were sufficient unto themselves, under the dominion of no one. This did not preclude them from using males for purposes of fertility.

That woman fears sex is undeniable. She has reason to do so. Her whole life may be changed by a sexual encounter in a way that a man's is not. In the words of the Abyssinian woman quoted by Kerenyi:

> ... the day when a woman enjoys her first love cuts her in two. She becomes another woman on that day. The man is the same after his first love as he was before. The woman is from the day of her first love another. That continues so all through her life ... She must always be as her nature is. She must always be maiden and always be mother. Before every love she is maiden, after every love she is a mother.[2]

I believe these words are basically true in the psyche of most women, but in modern society the fear is increased by the slur and the ostracism which, though certainly less than before, is still put upon illegitimacy. Since the advent of Freud, man's whole attitude towards sexuality has begun to change. It seems that he has more or less digested the apple from the tree of knowledge of good and evil given him by Eve, and, stretching out his hand to the same tree, he has plucked a second apple and this time it is he who has offered it to her. He has discovered the contraceptive.

By so doing he has opened to mankind a vast new world of consciousness. By its means men and women alike are enabled to plumb greater depths of degradation than ever before, but also to touch spiritual heights which had hitherto been reserved for the fortunate few.

It was Eve who freed Adam from the blindness of nature. Now Adam has freed Eve from the inexorability of its rhythmical wheel. Like the first apple, the second has opened vistas more far-reaching than a changed attitude towards sex.

Eve has been avid in her eating of this newest stolen fruit. Her energy, once locked (not necessarily unhappily) in an endless chain of bearing and rearing children, has been freed for pursuits

[2] Jung and Kerenyi, *Essays on a Science of Mythology*.

of every kind. She has both soared, and elbowed, her way through thick and thin, filling her lungs with her new found freedom till Adam, and sometimes Eve herself, must have wondered if he had been wise to let her taste that second apple.

But once tasted there is no going back, and now it is woman's turn to shoulder a genuine sense of guilt. The contraceptive is for her a sin against nature in a way that simple sexuality never was. It is in line with the whole modern search for an illusive ideal of security. Our effete society is riddled, it is rotted, with the idea of playing safe. We insure against every risk. Even our love is pressed into the same ignoble pattern. 'Use Durex and be safe.'

To a deep layer of the feminine psyche this is abhorrent. The fact that medicine has made childbirth relatively free from danger does not liberate woman from her innate willingness to risk her life. Love which does not risk all is sadly lessened. And if risking all entails pregnancy, the basic woman is ready to risk her life again in birth, or if need be, in abortion. To 'play safe' is the one thing that those women who are in touch with their feminine nature cannot do, without leaving some trace of guilt in their psyche, however buried in the unconscious this may be.

But the apple has been eaten and there is no going back. Now she also is burdened with the sin entailed in choice. Hitherto, unless she eschewed nature altogether to become a nun, she had virtually no choice. Biology and racial needs had held her firmly in Nature's grip.

This is not quite true. There was always a narrow door of escape for the most daring from a continual round of procreation, through abortion. I cannot prove this but I suspect that abortion must have been practised from time immemorial. Literature abounds with references to the old woman down the side alley to whom girls resorted when in trouble. And presumably these old women were descendants of witches who carried out abortions behind the back of the Church and overstrict husbands in the same spirit as they administered love potions.

Curiously enough I believe that abortion is far less obnoxious to women than to men, provided of course that it is the woman herself who rejects the child and that she is not being forced to rid herself of a baby she really longs to have.

To the Church and to civilized man the destruction of a life that has already begun seems to be more heinous than to prevent conception. But I am not at all sure that this is true of woman's basic instincts. Doubtless men resent the casting out of 'their' seed by a woman. But to her the sacredness of the man's seed only applies if she loves him. The deeper her love, the more total is her acceptance of the new life. But where there is no love she is singularly unsentimental about life. For a great many women a foetus of only a week or two holds no emotional appeal. Death in any case is part of life. Woman, who is so intimately and profoundly concerned with life, takes death in her stride. For her, to rid herself of an unwanted foetus is almost as much in accord with nature as for a cat to refuse its milk to a weakling kitten.

It is man who has evolved principles about the sacredness of life (which he very imperfectly lives up to) and women have passionately adopted them as their own. But principles are abstract ideas which are not, I believe, inherent in feminine psychology. Woman's basic instinct is not concerned with the *idea* of life as such, but with the *fact* of life. The ruthlessness of nature which discards unwanted life is deeply engrained in her make-up.

Modern woman is of course far removed, in her image of herself, from ruthless nature. Civilization depends upon overcoming nature. If Eve had never tempted Adam with that first apple there would have been no civilization. But tempt him she did, and woman also became civilized. I have, however, been struck by the spontaneous reaction of many women and young girls to the thalidomide tragedies. So often I have heard them exclaim with absolute conviction, 'Of course they should be aborted! It is criminal to make a woman carry a child which she believes may be deformed.' They have gone further and declared, when once their attention was drawn to the problem. 'It is monstrous that man should decide whether a woman should or should not have her own baby.'

This is not Christian morality. It is a spontaneous expression of Nature's law, which has its own morality. Although Nature may often have to be overcome, we ignore it at our peril.

Now what is the effect of an abortion upon a modern civilized mother? For years I have been much concerned at noticing the disturbances caused by past abortions upon the minds of my women patients. I had thought that this was due to the abortion itself which I had assumed was contrary to women's psychological make-up. But recently I have become overwhelmingly convinced that the bad and lasting effect upon the woman is not the fact of the abortion itself but is artificially induced by abortion laws. If my contention is correct that abortion has from time immemorial been part of women's lore, its possibility must be inherent in the deep layers of a woman's psyche.

Abortion was doubtless made illegal in an honest attempt to safeguard the lives of women who suffered at the hands of abortionists with insufficient skill and no hygiene, as well as to satisfy the moral qualms of the Church.

Women today however are less in need of protection than of help. More and more they are becoming conscious individuals, no longer content to be solely occupied with procreation. They are conditioned and educated to play their part in society as a whole; and within their marriages tend to be as much concerned with being their husband's companion as mother of his children.

Family planning has come to their aid. It is recognized and respected in all walks of life. Even Roman Catholics, who are not allowed to use mechanical contraceptives, plan their families in so far as possible by use of the so-called rhythm method. Yet the moment, through some miscalculation, pregnancy actually occurs, a woman finds herself suddenly trapped in an impossible emotional situation by our antiquated abortion laws.

But there is many a woman of the highest calibre, physically strong and mentally balanced, who feels that a child is undesirable. She may be unmarried and consider it actually wrong to bring a fatherless child into the world. She may be already the mother of several children, and for the sake of the other children feels that another baby is more than she can cope with. It may be for the sake of the husband who also deserves attention yet gets very little in these servantless days when the wife is constantly tending a young baby. Love itself may sometimes demand the denial of nature. But whatever the reason, such a woman on becoming pregnant feels completely trapped.

Although abortion laws are being relaxed, there are still many areas in which the law does not allow her the common-sense solution of speedily terminating an unwanted pregnancy unless to continue it will endanger her life or health. This includes mental health. Provided a woman shows signs of mental breakdown the termination is legal.

The doctors cannot help her. No matter how sympathetic they may be their hands are tied by the law. Two things can, and do happen; if she is determined enough the woman may risk her life or health at the hands of some illegal abortionist and face the possibility of prison if it is discovered. Or she may go from doctor to doctor all of whom may agree that she is being perfectly reasonable, but are only able to pass her on to someone else, until the suspense has reduced her to a nervous wreck. Not until this has happened will she legally qualify to have the termination of pregnancy for which she has pleaded. Once she is officially in danger of a mental breakdown she can get an abortion legally.

And what, I ask, is the final result of such a course upon her marriage? The effect of this struggle is not being adequately faced by men. A woman's need is for mind and body to work in harmony together. In a gladly accepted pregnancy this happens.

A woman on the other hand who is determining *not* to carry an unwanted child is split in two, her mind refusing to follow the dictates of her body. Every day's delay accentuates this split. The obstacles put in her way permeate her with a guilt which is not basically hers, but is projected upon her by society. On the other hand every day the foetus which she could have aborted lightly with no harm to herself and without offending her nature, is nearer becoming a child who claims her love. Less and less is she clear what path is right. Society says to abort is a crime — while, to her, to bring into the world a child, of which in her heart and mind she has tried to be rid, is just as immoral.

The split and confusion widens until she either breaks down mentally and is granted a legal abortion or, as a last resort, she obtains one illegally. In either case she has ceased to be the normal balanced woman she was before the struggle began.

I am convinced that from this artificially induced split many a woman never recovers. When in later life it is seen that she has become frigid, or some other marital disharmony has appeared, the blame is put upon the termination of pregnancy itself. I emphatically refute this. The blame should be laid squarely where it belongs, on antiquated abortion laws with all their consequences; and it should be fully recognized that husbands eventually suffer as deeply as their wives. If only for the sake of her marriage a woman must be allowed to decide herself whether or not she will carry a child. It is an insult to her that a man-made society should make this decision for her.

In a society where women are given equality of education and of status, and where they are expected to take responsibility for earning their own living and to share in civic duties, it is wholly incompatible that in the realm of childbirth, which is so particularly and intimately woman's concern, she is still subject to laws which abrogate her personal responsibility. This is an indignity which she should no longer be asked to suffer.

So far I have spoken of the effects upon women of our abortion laws. But what of the unwanted child the less determined woman is forced to bear? It has become an accepted fact that unwanted children are the seed bed from which delinquency and much unhappy neurosis springs. Yet every year the state insists on the birth of thousands of unwanted children and sees no discrepancy between these two facts.

I am told that many women who would have gladly relieved themselves of an undesired pregnancy if it had been easy to do so, become devoted mothers in the end and are glad that they went through with it. I know this is true but I find it quite irrelevant as an argument for denying abortion.

I personally should like to see the responsibility for bearing children put upon the women themselves. Undoubtedly many women, married and unmarried alike, would decide to terminate their pregnancies and might, in later years, weep bitter tears of regret. We only learn from our mistakes. To me it is emphatically not the business of the law to save a portion of our less wise women from making their own mistakes.

I look for the day when women may both carry and keep the illegitimate babies they may have wanted without social stigma, and also take full responsibility for *not* bearing unwanted children.

I am not suggesting that abortions should be carried out lightly but only after learning from the doctor and the psychologist or the priest all the pros and cons. Our doctors are in fact in as much need as the women to be freed from laws which over and over again oblige them to act (or refrain from acting) in opposition to what they recognize would be best for a particular woman or a particular marriage. If the laws were changed the doctor could warn husband and wife of all the dangers, both physical and psychological, which may be incurred by an abortion and offer his advice, yet leave the responsibility of final choice to the woman herself. I do not underrate the importance of the father's wishes, but it is the woman who carries the child in her body and it is *her* attitude during pregnancy which will affect the child throughout its whole life. So the ultimate decision should, in my view, rest with her.

G

With the freedom to choose her own sexual life the burden of sin is already fully woman's own. She must be allowed to carry her choice through to the end. This is paradoxically her psychic pregnancy from which there is no escape: that she shall become a conscious and fully responsible being. Adam has already given Eve the second apple. Once tasted it can never be taken back.

# VII

# *Bridges*

FEW DAYS PASS in which I am not concerned in some way or other with the man-woman relationship; and every day I become less sure of the answers. The only certainty I have is that since no two people are alike, relationships between them are bound to be dissimilar.

With the rapid growth of consciousness of today, while women have developed their masculine creative side and entered man's outer world whether of action or of thought, men have become more receptive and sensitive to a sphere beneath the surface where women had hitherto been apt to dwell alone, albeit silently and only half aware. Only artists have hitherto been in touch with the feminine world.

This penetration by each sex of the other's realm has progressed so far that to speak of a man-woman relationship as though it were something definite is beyond me. As I once heard it half humourously put, there are no longer two sexes, but six. There are men,. women, homosexuals and lesbians, and there are also bisexuals and neuters. These physical and psychological anomalies and divergencies must never be forgotten for they are much more common than would appear on the surface. I must needs talk about the norm but I have never met it.

I have called this chapter Bridges because my contention is that a free relationship demands some degree of separation between individuals.

When people fall in love with one another they are so completely entangled that to tear them apart is like tearing a living creature asunder. Together they are a whole, separate they are two bleeding, mutilated halves. This vision of shared wholeness is known to us all but few of us are allowed to keep it for very long. This is not what I mean by a free relationship.

Relationship is a cold word. It has no vibrancy like, for instance, kinship, which immediately stirs something in one's blood, or like love with its infinity of overtones. It may mean great things

or almost nothing. Every encounter with a member of the other sex
can become some sort of man-woman relationship, and I am here
going to treat the man-woman relationship very broadly to cover,
for instance, my own friendly relationship with my gardener,
pleasantly and mildly coloured by the fact that he is a man and I a
woman, as well as the most intimate relationships between the
sexes.

I am not equating relationship with love. I am not going to talk
about love. Love is, I believe, something quite different. One can
build a bridge of relationship but one cannot build love. In the
richest relationships it will certainly be present but even when it
vanishes temporarily or permanently, a valuable relationship may
still exist. Love is greater than any bridge. I talk about love later in
another chapter.

In considering the bridges between two separate people I ask
myself how we can prevent ourselves from undermining the
bridges we have so painstakingly built. I am hoping you will forgive me if I talk more about the woman's end of the bridge than
the man's. I prefer to talk of things I know directly.

About the original difference between a man and a woman
there is one inalienable fact which we cannot escape: the girl baby
emerges from a being which is like herself. Being born, traumatic
as that must be for any baby, is for a girl nonetheless a continua-
tion of her identification with mother. Physical separateness goes
along with a psychological identification which lasts for years.
Mother lives again in the daughter and the little girl lives mother's
life and shares her activities from the moment she can act at all.
They are even in love with the same man.

The small boy on the other hand emerges from a being who is
different from himself. The first person he recognizes is also
mother, but from the very beginning of awareness he is clearly
different from her and his interests are different too.

Simone de Beauvoir's contention that the difference in psychological attitude of boys and girls is due solely to difference of
upbringing and expectations of the parents, seems to me, in part at
least, to be belied by these elementary facts. The difference in
attitude of boys and girls is visible almost from the outset.

I have seen a baby girl aged three months quiver with excite-
ment as she lay beneath an apple tree in blossom, while her
brothers of the same age were already fascinated by moving
wheels which left her comparatively indifferent. I knew one little

girl, who, at the age of two and a half, was so aware of her feminine role that when one day a man came to the house who did not respond to her flirtatious glances, she remarked to her mother on going to bed, 'Funny man. *Looks* like a man!'

This original difference of being different from or similar to mother, probably implants in the minds of men and women a pattern which appears in later life as an unconscious assumption of what relationship should be.

Women tend to seek identification with the person whom they love. A woman likes to follow her man and will even change her political ideas or her religion in her attempt to achieve once more that sense of union with another that was hers in the beginning. Even the modern woman who consciously admits a man's right to live his life without accounting for every moment of his day and expects to do the same herself, still wants to share his inmost thoughts and feelings, for that to her is the essence of true relationship.

Not so man. For him, separation is inevitable, and it is from his island of separateness that he tries to relate. For him the woman's attempts to probe the inmost recesses of his mind feels, consciously or unconsciously, like a threat to engulf him. He often feels her to be a siren from the deep luring him within her coils, or a gigantic white-crested wave which may submerge him. A woman finds it difficult to understand why he feels threatened. She herself rides the wave so easily. She has never been wholly separated from the water in which she floated at ease within her mother's womb.

Man has pulled himself out of the unconscious matrix with the effort of thousands of years. But his rational supremacy is somewhat precarious and he rightly fears to be submerged again. So, as often as not, he avoids emotion and teaches his womenfolk to do likewise. A man does not understand that a show of emotion on the part of a woman does not have the devastating effect on her that it has on him.

Women are most at home when ankle-deep in the unconscious. They can handle emotions. For them a burst of anger clears the air, and a flood of tears is the storm which releases thunderous tension and leaves them calm. The woman, who, in her desire for identification with her man, represses emotions as he has done, deprives not only herself but him as well.

Again and again I am surprised at the determination with which some intellectual men try to educate their wives to be as rationally minded as themselves, only to turn on them when they have succeeded. Such a man, and I am constantly meeting them, is really trying to turn his wife into another man. It may be that he is not yet mature enough to be able to relate to his opposite so he seeks in his wife the easy companionship which people of similar tastes and ways of thought can share. It is not till he has achieved this happy condition that he realizes that something is missing and blames his wife for his own mistake. A woman who has lost all her native contact with the irrational has ceased to be herself and is no longer the woman who originally met his need. The opposite situation where a wife drags her husband into her own emotional sphere, though luckily less frequent, is even more disastrous, for the man is brought to the verge of breakdown.

There are other men, on the contrary, who have such a large ingredient of the feminine in their own make-up that they seek a woman with a well-developed masculine side in order to encounter their opposite; but this, unlike the case where the man tries to make the woman like himself, may be one of those modern reversals of role between the man and the woman which are inevitable in this generation. It is not necessarily a sign of immaturity.

Now about the bridges. Any interest which two people share clearly forms a bridge on which they can meet. This is so obvious that we tend to put the cart before the horse by substituting all sorts of interests shared for the emotional bonds which are lacking. It is not uncommon, for example, for women to watch football Sunday after Sunday though it bores them to death. But such frail bridges easily totter. Men on the other hand seem less willing to suffer boredom for the sake of relationship and perhaps rightly so.

Ultimately of course communication in some form or other is the fundamental foundation for any kind of stable bridge. But communication does not necessarily mean talking things over. Spontaneous reactions are more likely to be valuable than studied words. Curiously enough talking is often one of our greatest stumbling blocks to mutual understanding. It sounds so simple, so easy to be frank and say what one means, but we so often omit to notice who in fact we are talking to. I would go further and say we are not always aware who is doing the talking. Neither party in a relationship is always him or herself, as everyone knows, but frequently forgets.

Endless confusion arises until one understands that there is no such thing as a simple relationship between one man and one woman. It is as though there were at least four personalities always involved, the man and his feminine side; the woman and her masculine side. (The unconscious of any ordinary masculine man is feminine in character and can be personified by the figure of a woman. Similarly the unconscious of an ordinary feminine woman is masculine in character and is personified by the figure of a man or a group of men.)

Though we do not usually think in these terms most people are very well aware of the phenomenon especially when things are not going right. For instance, when a man becomes moody and irritable, without giving one any idea of what is the matter, it will be because the feminine in his unconscious has for the time being taken charge of his personality. He is at that moment as incapable of expressing his real feelings as any shy girl; although it is also from the feminine in himself that a man gets his inspiration, he, the man, providing the form in which the inspiration will be expressed.

Inability to find words is one of the outstanding characteristics of the feminine. Some women have the greatest difficulty in expressing verbally their deepest thoughts and feelings. This may sound nonsense for women are proverbial talkers. But the loquacious woman, whether intellectual or not, is in reality as possessed by her masculine side as the moody man is by his feminine.

So long as this masculine, discriminating side is actively and fully employed by a woman all is well. She will be efficient and creative. It is when purpose is lacking that the masculine in a woman becomes negative. If then he turns his attention outwards she will make those sweeping generalizations that ruin general discussion, or throw out remarks which sound all right but which are actually just beside the point, causing unwitting havoc in the thinking of all around her. This constantly happens when the real inner woman is secretly concerned with some other matter much nearer her heart, when she should have known that she was really bothered inside about something quite different from the words her lips are uttering, and have remained silent; or have admitted to herself that the matter in hand was something about which she knew very little and that her contribution could be nothing more than opinions she had picked up from newspapers, or mere

reiterations of what her parents used to say. If she would learn to
listen to herself she would be surprised to find how often her obser-
vations are no more than this.

When a woman hands herself over to her masculine spokesman,
while the real woman in her retires into her own inner sanctuary,
cliché after cliché may even come rolling out in a voice vibrant with
emotion and then her husband or lover will probably end by
walking away and slamming the door.

On the contrary when the real inner woman is present in the
situation, her masculine side can express what she, as woman,
really means. This is not nearly as easy as it sounds, for women are
so educated to think and behave like men today that they are in
constant danger of losing touch with their own real inner truth. It
is very serious when woman's negative masculine side has no
external outlet at all for his energy. Then he will turn on the
woman herself. He will convince her that she is useless, and that
her life past, present and future, is utterly devoid of meaning.

Other misunderstandings between men and women are apt to
occur when one of the four personalities of which I have spoken is
absent. A man who tries to communicate with a woman without
the aid of his feminine feeling to make the bridge and enable him
to meet her on her own ground, is likely to produce a dry intellectual dissertation which either paralyses her or makes her angry,
according to temperament. Similarly, the woman who assumes
that her man will know what she is feeling without her telling him,
because to her it is quite obvious, has omitted to utilize her own
inner masculine clarity to convey the message, and leaves her
actual man bewildered and in the dark.

I have often wondered why women are more tolerant of a
man's moods than he of her irrelevant vocal outbursts. Perhaps it
is because a woman at heart tends to think of men as little boys,
and after all one can be tolerant of little boys. Moreover she
understands irrational moods and caprices. They are qualities she
not only recognizes in herself, she deliberately uses them to her
advantage when it suits her to do so. She is so familiar with their
fickle transitoriness that she can afford to greet them in her man
with a shrug of the shoulders, and wait for the mood to pass.

The man on the other hand is really put out by her clichés.
They shatter his clarity of thought because they lead him astray by
their very nearness to the truth. And perhaps, I suggest this with
all temerity, perhaps men are unaware how often they too are just

off the mark themselves. It is the things we are unaware of in ourselves which make us so very angry when we see them in other people.

As I have already said, in our present transitional stage no one quite knows his or her role. A man no longer knows what part in life he is supposed to take. Young men today constantly feel quite shattered by this uncertainty for both at home and in the outside world the roles of man and woman have been made to overlap. On the other hand I constantly meet the wife who has become ousted from her own kitchen, or is so organized by her husband within her own realm that she feels completely depotentiated as a woman. Her life becomes deprived of purpose, and without purpose she can no more live than can a man. Her only refuge is to join the ranks of her career sisters, a solution which is as likely to aggravate the problems between husband and wife as heal them.

In casting her net in wider waters modern woman has caught not only the fish she sought but a devouring monster as well which is busy destroying the more feminine among her number. Woman's invasion of man's sphere has, I believe, aroused in man's unconscious the determination to maintain his former superiority at all costs, even among those who consciously believe in and are most vociferously in favour of equality between the sexes. Consciously men welcome woman's emancipation but in the unconscious they despise her and are determined to keep her in her place. As one young woman I know puts it, 'Men like us to be creative because that is what makes us interesting, but they hate us to create as that's trespassing on their preserves.'

It is the *un*consciousness of this resentment which shatters the woman for it is picked up by her in her *un*conscious where it fortifies her own doubts of her own powers. It appears as a masculine voice which reiterates over and over again in a half-caught whisper or a resounding shout, 'You cannot do it, you are no good.' I have yet to meet the woman who is not familiar with this voice. A woman can in her own obscure way counter a man's open opposition. It puts her on her mettle. As my old mother used to say, 'One can't knock one's husband down but one has got to get round him somehow.' But antagonism when hidden can neither be circumvented nor dissolved. It reinforces all women's internal doubts and is, I am convinced, responsible for endless frustration and even breakdown on the part of women. This is the devouring

monster she has caught unwittingly in her emancipated net. It
silently destroys every bridge that men and women try to build.

However this may be, for any real deep communication to take
place between two people of the opposite sex, all four personalities,
two in the conscious and two in the unconscious, must always be
present at the same time. This is true whatever admixture of masculine and feminine there may be in each individual.

The most powerful bridge of all, is of course sexuality, but it is
not always such a firm safe structure as it would appear to be. It is
a common enough experience for a man and woman each to step
upon it from his or her own side of the river only to find that it
breaks in the middle throwing both partners into a stream tur-
bulent with frustration and resentment.

One partner may dash too quickly across the bridge to find that
the other has disappeared. The woman perhaps was not really in
her body at the time after all, or her body was not ready, so there
was no encounter; or a premature ejaculation overtakes a man,
breaking the bridge before it could be crossed. Each will return
sadly to his or her own domain whenever either party is for some
reason unable to meet the other spiritually as well as physically. I
am sure this is true of both men and women.

I am speaking of course of a real relationship. There is no bridge
and no relationship in shallow experimental physical encounters.

But in this field we are up against faulty education. Women
tend to believe quite erroneously that a man only wants her body.
Early warnings, newspaper reading and novels all help to incul-
cate this mistaken idea which is picked up by an inner voice and
whispered into a woman's ear at the most inappropriate moments,
turning her suddenly into a baffling icicle when all her warmth
had actually been needed. On the one hand she is taught from
infancy that man is a dangerous animal creature who is to be
trusted at her peril, inculcating fear on the physical level from the
start. On the other hand she is *not* taught that he is in fact dangerous because his truth and hers do not necessarily coincide, so,
unprotected and unwarned, many a woman allows herself to be
raped intellectually and spiritually over and over again.

I use the word rape deliberately for completely helpless children
are impregnated by immature adults with false ideas. On those
girls who have not been specially gifted with independence of
mind this crime is perpetrated over and over again. Unknowingly

they nurture such false ideas with their life's blood and finally bring forth monsters. As an example of what I mean: the educated women today who are so strenuous in their advocacy of physical punishment for juvenile offenders have obviously been raped in their childhood with the idea that vengeance is synonymous with justice, an idea which has ousted their innate protectiveness of the young wherever found. Any girl who grows to womanhood without knowing that love is her supreme value has been spiritually raped. Justice is one of our noblest concepts, yet the woman who would deliver up her husband, lover or son for the sake of justice, no matter what crime he had committed, would, to me, be a woman only in name. And I am sure that most women would agree with me.

The sensitive boy and man no doubt suffers, just as acutely. His struggle to retain his hold on his own truth may be even harder, because the expectations of society that material success should be his inevitable goal and physical sport the route to attain it, weighs upon him even more heavily than upon a girl. Nonetheless his innate power of discrimination is more likely to save him from the dire consequences of mistaken education. He may suffer outrage but he is less likely unknowingly to nurture monsters. Though admittedly he sometimes does so.

However this may be, a girl needs to be warned of her two-fold danger: one that the fear of physical rape is so deeply inculcated that it may lurk beneath the surface long after she has rationally dismissed it; and two that her real danger is in that most unsuspected place, her mind and her very soul.

As a rule a man has no conception of the basis of woman's fears nor of the inner voice that repeats them to her. For him sexual intercourse will in itself restore any broken harmony. He has no idea that for a woman a bridge of spiritual attunement must first be built before she is able, not willing, but able to trust herself to cross the bridge of sex.

Another aspect of woman's confusion is brought about by her modern education. Men's modern problem is apparently the separation of spirit and body. To what extent the Church has inculcated this split in man's psyche I cannot judge but it is unquestionably there as every analyst can testify.

The fact is that modern women have been brought up in this same school of thought where things of the mind and spirit are honoured and the functions of the body are debased, while our supreme gift of physical creativity is relegated to shady stories and lavatory jokes. Even the natural process of menstruation is called 'the curse'.

This divorce of mind from body pertains in girls' school nearly as much as in boys' so that women also tend to put the mind on a pedestal and at best their own bodies on the same level as that of cows or rabbits. Only the very feminine girl escapes this innuendo underlying her education. For most women very considerable experience of life is needed to grasp the truth for which they had been completely unprepared: that for the whole woman there is no possible cleavage between spirit and body, for it is in her body that her spirit dwells.

This discovery can come upon her like a revelation, and once understood, her inhibiting fear that man only wants her body vanishes into thin air. She can abandon herself as never before in the physical encounter for she knows that if he can meet her in her body he cannot fail also to find her spirit.

But neither partner must ever take the other for granted. The bridge may be strongly built, but leave to cross has to be asked and granted anew each time. This applies throughout all the sphere of the man-woman relationship, not only in matters of sex. Nothing is so disheartening as being taken for granted, day after day and year after year, whether it be the woman who takes for granted that her man will provide the money or he that she will cook the supper. Taking for granted is of course more likely to happen in marriage than in other relationships, but wherever it happens, it stultifies the imagination and turns the relationship into a suffocating prison.

For thousands of people marriage has become a prison, and I want to look a little closer at this phenomenon to see if we can understand what has happened.

The determining factor is what goes on in the *un*conscious, for the unconscious is the source of dynamism, whether for building or destruction, not our conscious rational intentions.

What in fact is the unconscious of both man and woman doing to marriage? Some force is certainly very busy breaking marriages up. Jung has suggested that the numerical preponderance of women in the modern Western world is partly responsible. He suggests that the thousands of women for whom no husband is available, try in the unconscious to devalue the marriages of their envied sisters with the secret aim of annexing their husbands for themselves. Jung maintains that the undermining process is so widespread beneath the surface that even wives are affected by it, till they too weaken the marriage bond in their lurking doubt whether after all marriage is worth the bondage.

But this explanation was written before the last war and it hardly seems adequate today, when the preponderance of women over men is rapidly righting itself. More deep-seated is, I believe, the growing desire to be free.

Women, still dazzled by the glitter of what they thought would be freedom promised by their emancipation, find themselves either pressed into the new unexpected moulds of our commercialized society or swamped by domesticity with no outlet for the talents modern education has fostered in them.

In either case they chafe and fret and, with their feminine subtlety of indirect attack and their capacity to close their eyes to what they do not want to see, break the prison that is nearest them and within their ability to break: the marriage of their neighbour or their own.

Jung's greatest plea for women is to learn to know their goal. What today is woman's goal? I believe few women have any idea towards what end they are striving. The unmarried certainly would not admit that they are trying to break the marriage institution, nor do wives admit that it is they who undermine the marriage walls. Yet marriage after marriage totters and becomes a shambles.

Doubtless another reason for this collapse is the decline of religion. The highest values of mankind today are without a home. The channel for man's mystical aspirations and his need to worship something greater than himself was hithero provided by the Church. Today man finds himself with no definite spiritual goal. The energy thus freed has been poured by men into the advance of science, or material progress or the State. But these gods are too impersonal for a woman to worship. If there is no God at least there is a man to love. So all her displaced energy flows into a man-woman relationship. There surely she will find her deepest values. This tenuous human relationship becomes her all. She fills it with her idealism, her expectations and her love. There is no limit to the value it is asked to hold.

Moreover contraceptives have freed immense energy which would otherwise have been used in bearing and rearing children. So the surplus energy of women is doubly great. When it all goes into the marriage relationship (which seems to many a woman to be the only place of value which is left to her) by the very frailty of its humanness the marriage bursts asunder and leaves her desolate. Maybe this tottering institution of marriage has, in its present rigid form, outworn its usefulness and we shall have to find new more flexible forms for those unions which also embrace a family.

Another mistaken orientation from which modern woman suffers is, I believe, the adoption of man's goal of independence. She thinks she *has* to leave home and lead a life of her own like a man. There is of course nothing against a woman living on her own if she wants to do so, and for some it is imperative, but the number of girls who pine in solitary studio apartments or furnished rooms, for no better reason than the assumption that this is what is expected of them, is tragic. More devastating than this chilly form of abode is the belief that it is essential for them to free themselves entirely from any inner psychological tie with their parents. This may be right for a man, but I am sure that there are many cases where it is quite unsound for a woman.

Women of one generation and the next overlap. It is as though there were a continuous rope of posterity running down through the women. And for a young woman to think she can opt out and deliberately cut herself off from this is often to belie her nature and enslave herself in an abstract theory. One modern very independent-minded young professional woman, who had been much preoccupied with what seemed to her a too close tie with her mother, said to me one day, 'You can't think what a relief it is to know I do not need to break with my mother, to know that it is through her that I am a link in a chain back into the past and forward into the future. For the first time I feel free.'

I have an uneasy feeling that the trend of today wherein women so largely live their masculine side in careers and jobs, and men have become correspondingly more sensitive and receptive, is hiding extreme danger under a deceptive appearance of greater wholeness in the individual.

There can be little doubt that with rare exceptions the masculine of woman is inferior in quality to that of a man. It is apt to be less original and less flexible. She tends to be impressed by organization and theories which she frequently carries to excess because her masculine power to focus runs away with her. She then becomes hidebound by regulations and obsessed by detail. She is much less likely to be willing to make exceptions than a man, as the masculine side which runs away with her is wholly impersonal and disregards the human need of any particular man or woman.

But the same sort of thing applies to the feminine within man. It is less vital and dynamic than that of woman. The feminine in women is not solely passive and receptive. It is also ruthless in its service of life, or rather of those particular lives which personally concern her. She is as ruthless as nature. There are no lengths to which a woman will not go to foster the welfare of her immediate family or those she loves. The feminine of man on the other hand is soft and gentle, lacking this ruthless service of life every bit as much as the masculine of woman lacks originality and flexibility.

Man's way of cherishing is to build a welfare state which will care for all: an admirable civilized institution but so depersonalized that in spite of the excellency of its aim, it appears to be in danger of sapping the will and sense of responsibility of the individual man and woman.

Like that of woman, the man's contrasexual side is always wholly impersonal. This is the thing to be remembered: the forces in the unconscious, whether in man or woman, hold the dynamism but are inhuman and impersonal.

Our task is to allow these dynamic forces to work through us (for without them we are impotent) yet to avoid being mercilessly enslaved by them; only so can we reduce their force to human proportions. To be human is our greatest need, and also the thing we find most difficult.

Take another quality: ambition. Without ambition it is doubtful if anyone would have the necessary drive to achieve any great work. Ambition is indispensable. It is one of the qualities of mankind which has helped to achieve our civilization. Ambition is, I should say, a masculine attribute whether found in man or woman. Nature is ruthless but in no sense ambitious. The apparently feminine woman who ceaselessly eggs on her man to greater achievement regardless of his own desires, is in fact unconsciously possessed by an ambitious masculine devil within her, which has got completely out of hand. It is when ambition is harnessed in the service of life that it furthers the development of mankind. Our enormous advances in medicine are notable examples.

Similarly, if men, without knowing it, are taken over by their negative feminine side in the form of vanity, they also become victims of inhuman impersonality. They are spurred on to ever greater and greater heights, and the needs of life are forgotten in the fascination of their own powers of creation. No matter that a quarter of our globe is starving and millions of refugees pine in camps; no matter that spiritual anaemia is rife throughout the world, the moon is conquered and mankind has won the power to commit racial suicide.

This state of affairs is probably the product of each sex being *invaded* by the characteristics belonging to the other rather than by being consciously and positively related to the opposite in themselves. Perhaps men are in the greatest danger here, for the age of enlightenment set reason on a throne. The resulting devaluation of the irrational feminine within man himself thus turned it into an enemy to be repressed rather than honoured as the essential other side of life. It is the repression of a dynamic force which renders it explosive.

Women on the other hand, have not in the past repressed their masculinity. It existed only as a potential. But, when unrelated to, it can also be a menace, though it has not the same terrifying disruptive lunatic force that the feminine has in man's psyche when it breaks its boundaries, as happened in the two great wars which were due mainly to the eruption of the repressed and dishonoured irrational feminine, gone mad throughout the world.

The prevalent unconscious contrasexual invasion within individuals is in a sense a set-back rather than an advance in maturity; though I have no doubt that it is a temporary and necessary stage which will be followed, if we survive, by an enormously enlarged awareness. It is, I hope, a case of *reculer pour mieux sauter*. The place to which we shall finally have to jump is a state of mind wherein the masculine and feminine are consciously experienced and related to one another *within* each individual rather than between two individuals of the opposite sex. At present this ideal is only the ultimate goal of a long life fully lived; if aimed at too soon the young may cheat themselves of an essential stage of their lives.

I have called this chapter Bridges. As man and woman have, throughout the ages, walked on either side of the river of life there have always been some bridges which have enabled them to meet. Mutual understanding may have been at a minimum but we have always been able to trust that devotion, passion and sexuality would throw bridges across the stream over and over again.

Mutual responsibilities with joys and sorrows shared have strengthened the foundations and built, stone by stone, bridges which could withstand storms and rushing torrents. But in the past each partner still dwelt on his or her own bank of the river.

Today it is as though the banks were crumbling, narrowing the river bed until it can be jumped across. Already I see in my mind's eye the sands from either side mingling and mounting slowly till they form a terra-firma on which anyone can walk in easy companionship.

But if this should happen, the dynamic river would have ceased to flow, dammed up by the mingling sands. How long, I wonder, would it be before the imprisoned accumulating weight of water crashed over us, drowning our endeavours towards equality in a gigantic bid for freedom to flow once more between two banks.

I believe we have it in our power to avert such a dread calamity if we will only learn that the opposites must always be separate if they are to be related.

Paradox is the essence of living. Perhaps the greatest paradox in man's psyche is our longing for union, for peace, for solutions, though experience has taught us that it is our conflicts and our failures which are in fact our points of growth.

We can throw bridges of understanding across the abyss between our hate and our love, our doubt and our faith and every other pair of opposites. And the mystic can doubtless at moments hold them all together, but to do so continuously is the finality of death.

Separation is the keynote of relating the opposites in life. It is the keynote of a free relationship between man and woman. But the separation of the past with a clearcut distinction between the two sexes, who were nonetheless joined compulsively to form one whole, is over. The present is a confused intermingling of male and female in both sexes which befogs relationships. Yet the future may hold some clarity where men and women may each relate to the opposite within themselves without women being swallowed by their masculine or men by their feminine characteristics.

I believe that ultimately we shall have to find wholeness within ourselves in order that we may walk along the river of life on either bank making relationships with individuals on the other side of like wholeness to ourselves. These meetings of whole people will surely take place on bridges which span the stream of life flowing between two separate banks.

H

# VIII

# *What Do We Mean By Love?*

MY DAYS ARE spent listening while people tell me their troubles, and as they all inevitably speak from time to time of love I have had much occasion to be astonished at the different meanings with which they endow the word. Men and women often see it from bewilderingly different angles, each speaking of love with complete assurance, unaware that it means something else to their partners.

I am not referring to the forms of love's expression. We are all familiar with its endless variations from the lowest to the highest. The confusion lies in what people think is the nature of love itself. Of this I have made no special study, except for my ordinary woman's preoccupation with love. I am merely feeling my way around the periphery of this great ball of light which seems to be at the centre of our lives, and voicing some of my musings.

I do not know what love is. When I was a girl of eighteen I had no doubts. I scorned books on love with impatience. It all seemed so simple. Words could do nothing but confuse and blur our innate clarity of direct vision. Words could do no more than provide a golden cage for a bird whose wings had been clipped, drooping in its gilded prison. I was very healthily aware of the danger of practising as Aldous Huxley puts it: 'Alchemy in reverse – we touch gold and it turns into lead; touch the pure lyrics of experience, and they turn into the verbal equivalents of tripe and hogwash.' That was at eighteen. But the further I have travelled, following as all natural women do the voice of love, the less sure have I become that I know anything about it at all.

Please notice that I am not writing about 'relationship' here, nor about 'sex', nor any other particular form or expression, but about love itself in whatever place or form it happens to alight on us.

Love is known by everyone, yet the direct experience becomes

so hedged around with assumptions that we get confused. And
then, when life disproves these assumptions, we begin to wonder
if the essence we thought we knew had only been a mere trick
of the light. Perhaps these assumptions are the gilded bars of the
cage.

The first of these popular beliefs, which is very soon and most
disconcertingly proved false, is that love is permanent. We assume
that the love between parents and children should persist, that the
love of wives and husbands should last their lives, that lovers
should be true unto death. Yet the permanence of love's presence
is an ideal which bears little resemblance to the facts. How many
children love their parents when they no longer need their care?
One has but to scratch the filial surface to find emotions very akin
to hate or a far more poisonous indifference. How many married
couples, at best, retain more for one another than tolerance, kind-
liness and sympathy? The divorce courts tell the tale of the worst.
How few of us are capable of being Tristans and Isoldes!

It is a pathetic disillusionment when we stare these facts squarely in the face. It seemed for a while that psychology was coming
to our aid when it said, 'Ah, those people you speak of never loved
at all. It was all a delusion, a mirage. Those cases were only
projections. The little child projects the unconscious in all its
power for good and evil on its mother. It projects the wisdom
of the ages on its father, and they in turn project their future,
their ambition and their immortality on their child. Men project
their inner image of woman on wives and mothers, and women
the spirit of culture and authority on their men.' 'Withdraw
your projections,' we were told, 'only then can you learn to
love.'

Learn to love? Was not that only another assumption? Another
bar of the gilded cage? Has anyone ever learned to love? We can
withdraw our projection certainly, and by so doing we can learn
to understand one another. But I do not believe anyone ever
learned to love.

Love happens. It is a miracle that happens by grace. We have
no control over it. It happens. It comes, it lights our lives, and very
often it departs. We can never make it happen nor make it stay.

In Christopher Fry's play *The Dark is Light Enough*, the
Countess in the last scene denies to Gethner that she had ever
loved him. He is incredulous, in view of all she has done for him,
but supposes her to mean that he never deserved her love.

She replies in these words:

> It never came about.
> There we have no free will.
> At the one place of experience
> Where we are most at mercy, and where
> The decision will alter us to the end of our days,
> Our destination is fixed;
> We are elected into love.

We can perhaps learn to prepare for love. We can welcome its coming, we can learn to treasure and cherish it when it comes, but we cannot make it happen. We are elected into love.

This is, I believe, equally true of every kind and degree of love, ·from the love that shines in a baby's eyes when it first really sees its mother and gives her a smile of recognition, through the whole gamut of intimate human relationships, both spiritual and physical, to the furthest extreme of impersonal love which we call Agape; of this the life of Christ is the supreme example.

Even this impersonal, healing love, some measure of which is attained by a few great spirits, is utterly beyond anyone's power to learn or to control. It also happens. No man can make love shine through his life at will, no matter how he strives. The striving may prepare the ground, but he can take no credit for the love. To that he was elected. It happened. To some it may come simply without apparent torment, and I would dare hazard that those through whom love shines most brightly are supremely unaware of it. Impersonal love is like humility. Those who have it do not think about it, much less talk about it. But in no case is there any choice, it comes by grace.

The young man does not choose the moment which transforms his life by love, nor can he choose the woman who evokes the transformation. The baby does not choose its mother and cannot withhold the love which is between them. Love simply happens.

Yet we take this miracle so for granted that when it has occurred we think it should be ours forever. May it not have been an attempt to soften our disillusionment at love's passing which made the psychologist in the past deny that it had ever been there when the young fall out of love? 'It was only an anima-animus projection,' they told us. But were they not themselves caught in the false assumption that love is permanent?

The miracle of being in love is too overwhelming an experience ever to be dismissed as a projection. I do not believe for one moment that a projection can in itself light up the whole world. It is the love which goes with it that lights the world.

I do not deny the projections, nor the need for them to be withdrawn, but if we do not honour love itself as also present during that brief time, I think we are wilfully blind and we belittle our human stature. When we allow this to occur we have entered the realm of the debunkers and handed our psychological tools to the devil.

Please remember that I am not attempting to make a distinction between different kinds of love: physical or spiritual love, Eros and Agape or any other classification. To me love is always the same wherever it appears. The differences lie in our capacity. Where love is, it is as though some presence had alighted, a third, a something else, a something greater than the little persons who are involved.

I find it easier to think of love as being present than to talk of loving. It fits better with my belief that love happens and cannot be taught or learned. It is a monstrous conceit to think we can teach a little child how to love. He knows. He knows far better than we disillusioned grown-ups. Even in the transient trustful smile a baby will give a stranger, something lights up and the stranger will go on his way feeling more vital and more at ease with himself. Was that not love? I think perhaps it was. But it didn't stay. The stranger and the baby met for a moment and parted. They had no further concern with one another.

In the home the presence of a child will normally bring love with it. There is no question of learning here, and I do not doubt the genuineness of the love. Yet this is the very place where we find one of the biggest and falsest of the assumptions which surround our common usage of the word love. The immense flow of libido of a mother towards her child occurs at the same time as real love, and in the mother's mind the two are synonymous.

But are they the same? Is a mother's instinctive care of her child necessarily love, or may it not sometimes be a flow of nature's milk of which she must rid herself as urgently as of an overcharged breast? Most assuredly it feels like love, this pouring of libido upon her child, but every psychologist knows how destructive it may be.

Mothers come off badly these days. They are told they devour their children, poison their lives, cripple their growth; yet in all sincerity the mother thinks that what she gives is love. Can love cripple? Can love poison? I do not believe so. Surely we have made some hideous mistake. We have assumed that giving must be love, and failed to notice that giving what is not needed chokes and hampers; it may even kill.

Woman needs to give. She cannot help herself. Life pours through her and she has no choice but to pass it on, or let it stagnate until it becomes an abscess in her breast. This flow of life is not intended only for her children, but also for her mate. But many a man is too proud to accept her giving, confusing it with the mother's milk he has outgrown, unaware that it is the water of life she offers him. So she, in desperation, pours all her libido upon her sons and daughters not knowing what she does, and wonders why they drown.

Some years ago I heard Michael Fordham[1] give a lecture that I have never forgotten in which he spoke of the reciprocal roles of parents and children. He said that little children, who are beginning to emerge from the sea of the unconscious, need their parents to be strong, firm breakwaters in order to prevent the ever-menacing sea from inundating them again.

And in exchange the child, by his strangely wise words and his unpredictable behaviour, can be a link between his adult parents and the unconscious from which they have themselves broken away; if only they will listen to him and notice what he does. But this denotes a constantly changing situation. As the child grows, linking up the tiny islands of consciousness till finally he is standing on a sizeable piece of land with an ego of his own, the need for his parents' breakwater becomes less and less. So also, as he withdraws himself from the enveloping sea, will his words and actions have less contact with the collective wisdom of the unconscious, and be less in harmony with his own instincts or the psychic situation of his father and mother, and so he will be less and less of a link between the unconscious and his parents. The attitude of parents to children must be changing all the time to meet this fluid situation, if some condition is not to arise which drives love out.

The problem of parents and children, however, is not merely one of reciprocity, but of each generation being in its right place in

[1] Michael Fordham, M.D., B.Ch., M.R.C.P., founder member of the Society of Analytical Psychology.

the chain of posterity. Every individual is so linked with the past through the parents and to the future through the children that it is difficult to remember that it is with our own lives that we are fundamentally concerned. We are very greedy of life and try to live through our children the life we have failed to live ourselves. This puts a terrible burden on the children, making them live out the unused talents or the unconscious desires of their parents. Many a young man finds himself impelled to be an artist or a writer, though he has no great aptitude, and when one looks beneath the surface one finds that a parent or grandparent had repressed real talent thus forcing its outlet upon some unfortunate descendant. In T. S. Eliot's *Family Reunion* the son Harry pushes his wife overboard without really meaning to do so, and only later discovers that he had unwittingly carried out his father's unadmitted desire to get rid of his own wife. All but Harry thought it was an accident.

In actual life one is constantly coming across such things, and it is brought home to me again and again that the sins of the fathers are visited upon the children unto the fourth generation. The real sin is the failure to be conscious where one is capable of being conscious. For it is unconsciousness which gives such libido to the repressed talent or desire that succeeding generations are forced to enact it. Harry would not have had to push his wife into the sea had his father been fully aware of his own desire and then consciously refrained from carrying it out.

This type of burden we put upon the young does not make for love. Neither does the weight of our advice. We forget that, though we have in fact gained a little wisdom from our experience, our children do not start as raw material waiting for us to mould them, but actually build upon the foundations we have laid. They start to a certain extent where we leave off and, from the very fact of being born later, are beyond us. The post-war generation of children are startlingly more conscious than their parents were and the children of parents who have made it their business to be conscious themselves may have been given a start which enables them to leap far ahead beyond those same parents. I am sure we should listen with respect to what the young say, just because they are young, if we would keep love between us.

In our rapidly changing social and psychological patterns, it is difficult to be adaptable enough to make the conditions in which love stays. The young man has always had to struggle away from his mother's influence; but when mothers are as well educated as their sons and turn themselves into the son's intellectual companion, the struggle is even more violent. Mothers are tenacious in a new way. I recall the young man who bitterly complained that although he had left home he could not escape his mother. 'It is terrible, she prays for me every day!' Yet what more natural, or even more laudable, than to pray for one's son? Perhaps the trouble was caused by the way she prayed.

If a woman prays for her son's welfare she may actually divert his fate. Things may even apparently go better with him. He may refrain from marrying the undesirable girl or making some apparently fatal mistake. And yet we know so little of the pattern that belongs to us, or to those for whom we are concerned, that our very intervention, though it be by heartfelt prayer, may be damaging. I suspect that this type of insidious intervention through the unconscious is more potent and far more dangerous than the visible interferences from which one can protect oneself. The good faith in which it is made does not guarantee its freedom from poison. The apparently undesirable girl may be the right one. Some disastrous mistake from which the fond mother tries to save her son may be the very mistake he needs to make.

Parents spend their lives trying to save their children from making mistakes. And yet, when we look back over our own lives, we can all see how fruitful our mistakes have been. The mother who prays daily for her son's welfare is still playing her protective role, still trying to be a breakwater. She is giving in excess of his need and the love between them vanishes. If she could only be content to pray that nothing be allowed to divert him from his true destiny, whatever strange course that might take, then I believe he would be strengthened and not shackled by her prayers, and love might remain between them.

If on the other hand the mother errs in the opposite direction her son may feel cast out and lost, and again love vanishes. Our modern overstress on independence may be one cause of the number of lost young men wandering about today.

To strike the balance and give enough, yet not too much, is immensely difficult. Perhaps trust is all a woman can safely give her children. Trust may be one of the vital conditions wherever we would have love stay.

Look for a moment at the other side of the picture. The parents are growing old and some son or daughter stays at home and cares for them, sacrificing his or her own future marriage or career to do so. Love may be present here, but often it is only duty masquerading in the guise of love, poisoning the atmosphere with repressed and hidden hatred and resentment. The child-parent roles have become reversed without the parents giving up their claim to be masters of the house. Change of attitude has not kept pace with change of need, and love has gone.

It is not easy these days for the aging to keep their right place in the chain. We need the ripe wisdom of the old. That is their culminating contribution. But science will not let them die naturally even when they are ready and longing to depart. This is called respect of life, but I sometimes wonder if it is not, in the words of Buner, 'Man's lust for whittling away the secret of death'. We do not honour death today. So the old are often too long with us, and their cruelly overstretched-out lives become a burden that is insupportable. Love goes, and I wonder if the old, when they have been pushed out from the wholeness of family life, are less able to die because of it. Love and death are strangely kin. To be cared for from duty only sterilizes. We need love to be able to die serenely.

Duty and love are miles apart. I remember the story of a woman who was about to embark on a mountain of family washing, gaily singing to herself the while, when her husband came in and seeing the pile of sheets and pants and socks upbraided her for failure to organize the children to help her more. 'They should all have their duties,' he said. To his surprise his wife burst into tears, abandoned the washing and rushed out of the house. When she returned several hours later, she explained to her bewildered husband that the word duty made her sick. 'Can't you see,' she said, 'that I work for you and the children all day long for love. There are no limits to what I can do for love, but from duty I cannot wash one shirt or cook one meal, and what I cannot do I will never ask my children to do. I do not want their help to be a duty. One day they will help me from love, and then I will accept it.' And one day, a good deal later, unasked, they did so. That woman may have been wrong in her educational methods, but she certainly knew the coldness of duty and the dynamism of love. This dynamic quality is surely one of the hallmarks of love. In the presence of love there are no obstacles man is unable to surmount.

Meeting the other's needs appears to me to be the crux of the matter. Between adults, as between parents and children, it is the same necessary condition for the presence of love. When two people fall in love (whether they be of the same sex or of opposite sexes is irrelevant in this connection) they find that the other somewhere meets their need and together they feel whole. But as each is growing all the time, every day the need is different. Those who are sensitive enough to notice the change of their own and their partner's need can change their attitude along with it. And if both partners are able to do this love may remain between them, or at least visit them very often.

It is those who fail to change with their own and their partner's changing need who fall so desperately out of love. A man may marry a woman younger than himself. To begin with all is well. He is the father on whom she can lean, she the daughter for whom he cares. But if she develops she will no longer tolerate being a daughter-wife nor need a father-husband. If he can sense this change and become the husband-lover, raising her from daughter to be his mistress-wife, then can love still be their constant visitor. Or, if an older wife can see her younger husband growing up and drop the mother role in time, she too may keep love within the marriage.

Please note I have used the word need, not want or desire. We may want things we do not need, and we are often unaware of our deepest needs.

But if either partner becomes possessive or over-zealous, or on the contrary too casual and unthinking, irritation and frustration creep in; the feeling of wholeness is destroyed and the relationship either breaks up, or hangs together merely from force of habit. But the love which was there has left it.

Love and wholeness go inextricably together. One may not be the cause of the other, but they occur together. And before there can be a wholeness there has always been a meeting, always an 'I-Thou' recognition.

I do not wish to give the impression that it is an easy matter to be at the service of another's need. It is difficult enough to know your own need, much more so that of another. The people who are always doing these things because they think it best for someone else generally go wrong, both for the other and themselves.

Paradoxically it is when we are true to our *own deepest* needs (not, I repeat, our immediate desires) that we are most likely to serve the other's need also. The mother who prayed daily for her son was following her desire and longing for his welfare, not her need nor his. Her real need was probably to develop a life of her own and, if she had done so, she would have served his need to be left free at the same time.

The man who stamps out some essential side of himself in order to meet his wife's need for a faithful husband, may cheat her of becoming, through suffering, a more conscious person which she may have needed to become; or he may poison the home atmosphere with his resentment at being warped. It is all heart-breakingly difficult. Mutual service without betraying one's own deepest truth is the paradox at the very centre of the art of living.

Unfortunately only one path to this central point is open to us. No one can know with any certainty the needs of another, but he can, if he will take the trouble, discover his own, and it is a fact that if a man will faithfully follow the path towards greater consciousness of himself, which means greater wholeness within, and at the same time maintain his willingness to serve his partner, he is likely to find he is meeting the need of that one also, and love will be between them. Wholeness is both the goal and the key. Consciousness is the tool.

In my belief it is the same love in every case. Whether we are floodlit or the recipient of only one ray, it is the same love. Love is all one. The difference is, as I have said before, in our capacity, but also in the direction and the emotion felt. Where two people are involved it is as though a spark flashed between their two opposing poles. This is a tension of high emotion, the love is *between* these two and we call it Eros.

But where the individual has found his relative wholeness within himself, the opposites meet *within* him; then there is no external tension and therefore no emotion. He may even be unaware of the love he radiates. This is Agape.

> The great of earth,
> How softly do they live;
> The lesser ones it is are praised,
> Revered;
> Still lesser, feared;
> But these,
> One hardly knows that they are there,
> So gently do they go about their tasks,
> So quietly achieve;

When they have passed,
Their life's work done,
The people look and say:
It happened of itself . . .[2]

To me it is man's task, his greatest task, not to learn to love, but to learn how to create the conditions in which love can alight upon us and can remain with us.

Within the regular patterns of relationship, parents and children, wives and husbands, we have at least precedent and instinct to guide us as to what the necessary conditions may be.

The supreme task comes in those relationships that have no set pattern. Here we have no guide and can only feel our way in each individual case, with unlimited patience and discernment and absence from preconceived ideas. For every relationship between conscious adults is unique, needing freedom to blossom into its own individual flower. We can only tend and cherish the bud with all our care, waiting for the flower to open and declare itself. We must never forget this uniqueness if we are to avoid being led astray by the advice or example of those who have gone before us, or by the teaching of psychologists who can no more know our particular pattern than we do ourselves. The outer form of such a unique relationship tells nothing of its significance. Its value lies in the quality of the meeting.

The tending of an individual flower of relationship may involve much heartbreak and endless sacrifice of personal desire. But even this must not be confused with love itself. Yet the degree of our faithfulness to the needs of a unique relationship, whose ultimate pattern we cannot know, is the degree to which love will shine through it. Even here we have no choice. We are elected into love. Our choice lies in rejecting or taking up the task.

When people speak of healing by love I always feel dubious, for so many things feel like love which may be something quite different. Pouring libido upon a person does not necessarily heal. It may bind with ever stronger silken cords from which there is no escape. I do not call this love.

Giving tenderness and understanding does not always heal. Sometimes it is necessary to have a heart of stone and let the sufferer beat his head against one's lack of comprehension until he has hammered out his own salvation. These things feel very far

[2] Written by Ruth Tenney, based on a poem by Lao Tze.

away from love, and yet the healer may be filling the necessary role so well that healing from within takes place. A wholeness may have been created between the sick man and the healer, or the wholeness may be within the sick man himself. In either case it is love which enters in and heals. For indeed I believe most firmly that the presence of love is the only healer. But let us not flatter ourselves that *we* have healed by love. Healing has happened by a miracle. The miracle is love.

In the analytical situation love is often present. I do not mean only the love of the patient for the analyst, which can so easily turn to hatred, and be just as effective either way. I mean the spark of some divine quality which enters in wherever there is healing, regardless of the specific emotion experienced in the analytical hour.

This is no merit on the part of the analyst. It is his job to keep himself as free as he can from making projections, while accepting the projections of his patient, in order that the channel of healing can remain clear and unobstructed. But when the analyst in rare moments of real healing speaks from the Self, and so speaks more wisdom than he can possibly have had, then love is present. Or when in the silence a flash of illumination suddenly breaks upon the patient, his heightened consciousness allows love to enter in. In either case it is the love which heals.

But it does not stay. There is something terribly hurtful in the word transference. It offends the dignity of the human soul to feel that the immense emotions felt in the analytical hour have been brought about in an artificial context. The transience of the analytical relationship can be wounding to the point of insult.

If we can grasp that love wherever it appears is real love; only that it does not stay when it no longer belongs to the situation, then we need not be hurt at the way love disappears between analyst and patient as strangely as it had come.

Nor should we forget that analysts are helped to stand the strain of their calling by the love which comes to them through the undemanding libido their more mature patients pour upon them. I am convinced that this gives them life and energy, whether they know it or not. This must be equally true of priests and every other kind of healer.

The love betweeen analyst and healed is, moreover, never only one way. A physician once said to me, 'One only loves those whom one serves.' And I am convinced that service, the willingness to serve, is one of the most important criteria for the presence of love.

The analyst certainly does serve. I would go so far as to say that unwillingness to serve is one of the basic causes of neurosis because it shuts love out.

Mutual need and willingness to serve are both inherent in the analytical situation. The patient needs the analyst, but the analyst most assuredly needs his patients, not only for his means of livelihood but also for his need to serve. You might almost say for his need to love, but more accurately for his need to be an instrument whereby love can enter in and heal. This is, I believe, the particular vocation of every healer.

What, I have been asking myself, is the situation in ordinary life where love is not returned? There seems no wholeness there. But if one looks a little closer, one sees that this is not so. Beatrice fulfilled the need of Dante by simply being who she was. He needed her as a focus for his adoration and a mirror for his soul. He adored her from afar and made no demands upon her. During her life he asked no more than a passing smile. And in the unpossessiveness of his giving he did not drive out the love to which he had been elected. I do not doubt that Beatrice was the richer, whether she was aware of it or not. It is our egotistical demands, our petty possessiveness, our stupid jealousies which turn a generous giving (one that makes the giver whole and enriches the recipient) into an irksome burden we try to cast aside. Then there is no love, only an abuse of giving, which is as tiresome as our demands.

Love is unique, and must never be confused with the many qualities which are inherent in a relationship. Tenderness, sympathy, understanding, patience, impatience too and anger, or even jealousy, are essential concomitants of relationship. None of these make love itself, not even all of them put together. A relationship has its own obligations and its legitimate demands, but, as one of my poems expresses it, love claims no rights:

> Let me hold a beacon in my hand
> Shining on your face alone
> My own in shadow
> Passion held in leash with pity.
>
> Let me clear the sanctuary
> Of money-lenders who would seek
> To strike a bargain
> And silence the raucous voice of duty.

> Let me break the chains that bind you
> Every claim the law condones
> Or my devotion warrants
> While giving you the freedom of my City.

We speak loosely of hatred as love's negation, but we all know it is nothing of the kind. Hatred is only the other side of the golden coin of love. One must be very concerned to take the trouble to hate. A novitiate once asked his master how many lives were necessary to reach Nirvana. The master answered, 'For he who loves God seven, but for he who hates God only three.'

That jealousy and love are wholly incompatible seemed to the girl of eighteen axiomatic. If one truly loves, one has no right to resent what gives the other happiness. When I was a child I heard these lines:

> True love in this differs from gold or clay,
> In that to divide is not to take away.

These words fell on my ear like a clarion call and have been a touchstone ever since.

But life has taught me that it is not as simple as that. Jealousy is not necessarily a mere egoistical desire to possess for one's very own, not just a selfish unwillingness to share. It is the anguish of despair; the wholeness one thought one had found with the loved one is shattered. The golden coin of love lies smashed to pieces at one's feet. One is overwhelmed with fear. But this is no cold, dank, cloying fear; it is burning with the intensity of one's desire for wholeness and one's desolation at its betrayal. It burns with a heat which can destroy, which can make Othello strangle his Desdemona. There was no love in that dark moment. Love had been driven out by Othello's blind jealousy.

But if jealousy can be made to see; if a capacity and willingness to understand dwell in the heart at the same time as one is torn to shreds by jealousy, then the agony of despair can be lifted to another plane where its white heat can fuse again the scattered pieces of the golden coin; can make possible the return of love through acceptance of one's desolation and the humility of forgiveness. Wholeness is restored, but this time the wholeness is within the sufferer himself.

Dark jealousy, though often base, must not be despised. Rather let us beware when jealousy is absent. It smacks dangerously of indifference. The man who is so tolerant that he greets his wife's confession of unfaithfulness with, 'All right darling, go ahead,' is likely to be a cold fish who will wreck his marriage through the very coolness of his objectivity. Nothing could be more hurtful than a lover who cannot be fired by jealousy. Understanding needs to be fused with intensity of feeling before any transformation can take place, any forgiveness of betrayal ring true.

Indifference is the poison which seals up every channel of dynamic growth. Indifference, not hate nor anger nor jealousy, but indifference, hiding beneath a cloak of culture and rational behaviour, is the negation of love. It is the rejection and total loss of the golden coin.

Indifference is our failure to meet the other; our failure to meet the situation; or our failure to allow the opposites to meet within us, with all the conflict that entails. Where love is, there has been first a meeting, always a meeting. Without a meeting of opposites there can be no wholeness, and no chance for love to break through.

At eighteen I knew, but could not say, that it was from God that love breaks through. It was a long time before I could bring myself to use the word God. It had been bandied about so lightly and with such dubious assurance by people who, in the eyes of a child, seemed to be very little in touch with God. So I have had to travel a long roundabout way, a voyage of exploration through an inner world of images. And there I have found and brought up to the light of day an image of wholeness where all the opposites meet, even the opposites of our tiny egos and the great unknown.

Jung calls this the transcendent function and names its goal the Self. We do not understand what this means either, but in our need to try to express our fleeting glimpses of wholeness we find, or rediscover, some symbol to denote this moment of transcendence. It may be the Christian symbol, it may be something else. But whatever form it takes, it is the image of totality towards which we aspire; the supreme place of meeting. And it would seem that this essence of wholeness touches us repeatedly throughout our lives, each time to the degree of our capacity, impelling us always towards itself. No matter what we call it, we experience this as love.

I am not equating love with the Self, though I am convinced that wherever there is love the Self, our symbol of totality, is the

I

link which holds the two who meet together. The meeting in every case is in the presence of the Self. When this is not so, what passes for love is something else. It may be lust, it may be duty. It may be greed or a false self-abnegation, but it is not love.

Neither am I trying to equate love with God. I do not know what God is. But I do know, and have always known, with that inner knowing nothing can gainsay, that love is more than the meeting. At the meeting is the presence of the Holy Spirit.

I know no more about love now than I did when I started to write this chapter, but in the course of my musings there have emerged a few of the conditions which, I believe, we must attain if we would have love with us more than as a flitting presence.

# IX

# *The Rainmaker Ideal*

IN THE SPRING of 1959 all over the world people were watching and waiting anxiously for news of one man whom most of us knew very little about. Thousands of Chinese troops with massive guns and aided by planes were searching for the Dalai Lama of Tibet who had taken flight. Could he and his small retinue escape? The chances seemed remote. Then the news came through. The Dalai Lama had crossed the frontier into India.

Later an astonishing article appeared in that most respectable paper, *The Times*. The correspondent hesitatingly pointed out that the escape had the semblance of a miracle: the mountains had been unseasonably shrouded in mist during the whole flight, a mist which rolled away the moment the Dalai Lama reached safety. Moreover, the writer had the courage to suggest that this apparent piece of luck may have been due to the person of the Dalai Lama himself. He quoted another instance where an important feast was being held, and told how, as he had looked anxiously at the great menacing clouds overhead, a member of the crowd had come up to him and said, 'There is no need to be so worried, it won't rain till the feast is over, there are several Lamas present.' And in effect it was not until the last richly robed participant had reached his home that the rain drenched down.

I suspect that many a reader of that article will have dismissed it with a shrug and the comment 'That correspondent has been out East too long.' But we can, I think, afford to regard this happening with a more open-minded sense of wonder; and though we do not understand it perhaps we can try very tentatively to grasp its significance.

The Dalai Lama's escape and the reputed influence of Lamas over the weather, bring to mind the traditional Chinese story of the Rainmaker which most of you probably know. In a remote village in China a long drought had parched the fields, the harvest was in danger of being lost and the people were facing starvation in the months to come. The villagers did everything they could. They prayed to their ancestors; their priests took the images from the temples and marched them round the stricken fields. But no ritual and no prayers brought rain.

In despair they sent far afield for a 'Rainmaker'. When the little old man arrived, they asked him what he needed to effect his magic and he replied, 'Nothing, only a quiet place where I can be alone.' They gave him a little house and there he lived quietly doing the things one has to do in life, and on the third day the rain came.

This is to me as profound a story as any parable of Christ and sets an example and an ideal which is a salutary complement to our Western passion for activity.

If only we could be rainmakers! I am of course not thinking literally of rain. I am thinking of those people (and I have met one or two) who go about their ordinary business with no fuss, not ostensibly helping others, not giving advice, not continually and self-consciously praying for guidance or striving for mystical union with God, not even being especially noticeable, yet around whom things happen.

Others seem to live more fully for their presence: possibilities of work appear unexpectedly or people offer their services unsought, houses fall vacant for the homeless, lovers meet. Life blossoms all around them without their lifting a finger and, as likely as not, without anyone attributing to them any credit for the happenings, least of all themselves. Rainmakers are very inconspicuous. It is easier to spot those around whom life withers. We all know the Jonahs in our midst, who, in our smug self-complacency, we cast into the sea.

Indeed, these rare people around whom life blossoms cannot be said to cause the blossoming. The Rainmaker of the story did not cause the rain to fall by the exercise of any supernatural power. Nor I am sure would the Dalai Lama claim that he had caused the shrouding mist to which he owed his escape.

The Rainmaker does not cause, he *allows* the rain to fall. Along with our ever-increasing knowledge by which we wrest from nature the secrets of the physical universe, make the earth more fertile, man more prosperous, and master diseases which attack us; we also erect barriers, block streams and poison wells with the one-sidedness of our understanding and the hardness of our hearts. We may even prevent the rain from falling.

We have forgotten how to allow. The essence of the Rainmaker is that he knows how to allow. The Rainmaker walks in the middle of the road, neither held back by the past nor hurrying towards the future, neither lured to the right nor to the left, but allowing the past and the future, the outer world of the right and the inner images of the left all to play upon him while he attends, no more than attends, to the living moment in which these forces meet.

In those rare moments when all the opposites meet within a man, good and also evil, light and also darkness, spirit and also body, brain and also heart, masculine focused consciousness and at the same time feminine diffuse awareness, wisdom of maturity and childlike wonder; when all are allowed and none displaces any other in the mind of a man, then that man, though he may utter no word, is in an attitude of prayer. Whether he knows it or not his own receptive allowing will affect all those around him; rain will fall on the parched fields, and tears will turn bitter grief to flowering sorrow, while stricken children dry their eyes and laugh.

This attitude of unvoiced prayer which wills nothing and asks nothing, exerts an influence exactly opposite in kind from the deliberate influence beneath the surface which is in constant use today.

There is a vast difference between allowing, and deliberately exerting power. I am not considering the obvious external uses of power, whether of physical force, the weight of general opinion, or the moral canon of the time. I am talking of power effected through the unconscious.

The technique of talking not to a person's conscious mind but direct to the unconscious itself is unquestionably an instrument of power, an instrument used by anyone who throws out an idea and does not follow it up with conscious discussion. The idea is heard and sinks into the unconscious, where, if it happens to fall upon fertile soil, it will take root and flourish and later emerge to the light of day as an idea which the person has thought for himself.

Prophets and teachers from time immemorial have used this method for communication. They have spoken to the multitude, not talked and discussed with conscious minds. The seeds have taken root and flourished. This is how conversions are made, never by argument and rational conviction.

Maybe our churches are so empty today because preachers increasingly talk to the conscious understanding of their hearers, forgetting, in this scientific age, that dynamism comes from emotions and ideas coloured with emotions in the *un*conscious mind.

Speaking to the unconscious is a form of communication against which it is difficult to protect oneself. Advertisers deliberately use this channel to influence and determine what people think and what they think they want. The daily press exploits it to the full in favour of political parties, while dictators and totalitarian governments are past masters of its use.

Speaking directly to the unconscious, bypassing the resistance of the conscious mind, is not necessarily harmful. It is a technique sometimes used deliberately by therapists and by innumerable women who have learned the art of getting their ideas across without arguing. This may be wise and beneficial all round but what a weapon it can become! Like everything else, in its very excellence lies its danger.

Quite apart from its tyrannous employment by dictators and advertisers, we can be unknowingly damaged by its subtle use in our personal relationships. How many men are undermined by the insidious dropping of unsound ideas by wives. In my experience even the most intellectual of men are not immune. How many women are crushed and diverted from their own true path by the insistent assumption of superiority which men let fall without intention.

It is not enough to have good intentions. Without greater consciousness than we normally possess of what we do and say, our good intentions can be the traditional paving stones of hell. But even when we are aware of what we say, the moment we try, through underground methods, to affect other people's thoughts or actions towards definite ends, no matter how alluring or how good the ends may seem, we have inadvertently taken the road that leads away from, not towards, the Rainmaker ideal.

It is for us to choose which way we will go; shall we go towards the exercise of personal power for preconceived ends (not necessarily egoistical ends, for the goal may be the common good); or shall we admit that being only human we do not and cannot know what the ultimate goal should be, and so rest content with working for our own individual poise in the hope that that will be the best way of allowing life to happen around us at its fullest?

Whichever way we choose, we certainly shall not get there by travelling in the opposite direction. If we want to go north we had better avoid the roads which lead south.

It needs a considerable degree of consciousness to avoid turning down the wrong road by mistake. It behoves us to examine the *direction* in which we are travelling: towards power in order to achieve preconceived ends or towards freeing those around us from our dominance in order to allow them to develop along their own lines.

To be a Rainmaker is, except for inspired moments, an ideal that is far beyond us, but ideals are ideals just because they are so nearly unattainable. They serve, not so much as goals to be reached, as lights on the far horizon towards which an occasional sign-post points. If we will follow these pointers I think we can be assured of following a direction which *cannot* lead to illegitimate exercise of power nor to any kind of dictatorship no matter how benevolent.

The remoteness of the ideal is daunting, for how in this complicated world can we influence or interfere with anything at all? Yet if one will only look a little more closely one sees that the outer world unquestionably responds differently according to our own frame of mind.

Take an everyday situation as seen by a shy person who comes to some group meetings. He may hide in a corner or sit in the front row, he will still be almost invisible. The chances are that he will creep away the moment the meeting is over in terror lest someone should speak to him, and still more alarmed at the prospect of no one speaking to him at all. Yet beneath his shyness may be hidden a very positive personality which he has not yet himself encountered. An analysis or some experience of life may bring out the hidden side and the next time he enters this same dreaded room of people he will be amazed to find, not only that his embarrassment has left him, but that the very people who never noticed him before actually speak to him of their own accord. They may even seek him out. Yet the only change in the situation is his own new self-assurance.

Everyone knows those horrible days when everything goes wrong. One just misses the train, one's boss is in a bad temper, the bus conductor is rude and the shop assistants refuse to serve one. If one is capable of being objective at all on such a day, admittedly rather a difficult feat, one knows that at the root of the trouble lies one's own negative mood. Like calls to like.

On the days when everything goes right it is easier to believe that it was entirely due to our own charm, skill, good taste and efficiency. We are apt to take even more to our credit than is our due, just as before we had taken the blame too little. Be that as it may, it is, I think, indisputable that our own inner mood had in both cases affected in some degree the way the outer world had received us.

If we can go as far as this in admitting our own partial responsibility for outer conditions we have already entered that path towards freedom where we need be no longer the blind impotent victims of our environment.

It is a very big step. Big because it is the first one, not because it takes us very far.

Unfortunately we can seldom change our mood by an act of will. But the simple recognition of its existence may enable us to laugh. Kindly laughter at oneself can be like bubbles of oxygen reinvigorating the air of a stuffy room.

In intimate relationships such as marriage it is fundamental to know that it is one's own inner attitude of mind which not only makes the room stuffy but actually influences the reaction of one's partner. For instance, the wife who complains of a bullying husband has generally brought it upon herself by a cringing attitude. In fact her own unconscious tendency to cringe will have caused her to choose a bully for a mate. If she can learn to stand up for herself it is extremely likely that, after the first shock of dismay at being thwarted, the husband's disdain will turn to admiration, even though he may keep his admiration to himself. The bully, whether it be wife or husband, and it is just as likely to be the wife, does not admire but despises the cringing victim.

Similarly the wife who despairs of her husband's inability to understand her, needs to recognize that she has not only failed to tell him what she means, she has probably failed to tell herself. Women's own confusion today about who they are and what they want of life causes a fog around them which confuses everyone. Far more important than an uttered declaration of her meaning is her own inner clarity.

Achieving inner clarity is I believe the prime task of both men and women. I have used the expression inner clarity before,[1] but I should like here to enlarge upon what I mean by it. May I try and explain my own homely imagery.

I like to think of every person's being linked to God from the morning of birth to the night of his death by an invisible thread, a thread which is unique for each one of us, a thread which can never be broken. Never broken or taken away, but a thread which can easily slip from our grasp and, search for it as we may, elude us.

Our bodies are at the lowest point of this thread which runs up through every sphere of heart and head and spiritual attainment. Still on our individual thread but beyond our human reach are, in my imagery, angels or demons which at supreme moments we feel we are able to contact. They are the intermediaries between us and God. To be on our thread is in Jungian language to be in touch with the Self, and the angels and other figures to which I refer are the archetypal images of the Self which all who have had an analysis learn to recognize. I am saying nothing new. I am merely using ordinary language to say the same thing both because I happen to like ordinary language and because it is only when I have put an idea in my own words that I feel I am beginning to understand it.

I am using the expression 'inner clarity' to mean conscious awareness of being on one's thread, knowing what one knows, and having an ability quite simply and without ostentation to stand firm on one's own inner truth.

It is when we are on our vital thread that life happens around us in a way that befits our individual destiny, for we have not interfered. This does not necessarily mean that everything happens as we would like. Misfortunes and mistakes are also part of our pattern. Even illnesses may be necessary from time to time to give us pause or teach us lessons we should not otherwise learn. But everything is meaningful and can be seen sooner or later to fit into the pattern of our lives. It is only when we have lost our thread that life seems purposeless, lacking in significance and unacceptable. I believe it is also an empirical fact that life happens more fully around those who are on their thread. So storms hold off or rain falls as is required. It was not in the destiny of the Dalai Lama to be captured by Chinese troops. He had no need to practise magic.

---

[1] 'Meeting' — Chapter 1.

It simply happened that the mountains were shrouded in mist until he escaped.

It is all very difficult, for to enter the road of allowing and freedom does not necessarily mean simple acquiescence nor inactivity. The Rainmaker may be an active person and a strong one. But he does not interfere, he does not block the paths. On the contrary, being primarily concerned with his own thread, his activities will be such as to come to him personally and belong to his own pattern. He is not trying to exert influence or to have power over others at all, not even in the unconscious.

His activity, when he is active, will be demanded of him by the dictates of his own inner truth. He only acts when failure to do so would be failure to be true to himself. For instance, a man sitting on the beach engrossed and profoundly concerned with solving an intellectual problem would not forsake his vital thread if he suddenly plunged into the sea to save a stranger from drowning; even though by so doing he lost the mathematical formula or the line of poetry which had been evolving in his head. It is more likely that he would have been untrue to himself had he been deaf to the cries for help. For some, on the other hand, action may be the predominant note of their lives and rightfully so. We cannot judge.

But whichever way it leads us, being true to oneself must never, never be mistaken for egoism. On the contrary the man who succeeds in maintaining contact with his own vital thread holds unceasingly in his heart the words, 'Thy will not mine be done.'

So long as we are in touch with this thread it is as though our individual Guardian Angel hovered above us guiding our steps. The moment we lose it we feel lost, purposeless and unsafe, shorn of the pristine magic which guards every small child. The little child, if he is allowed to follow his instinct, encounters danger again and again and miraculously survives. For the thousand or so children who are killed or maimed on the roads, millions just escape the whizzing wheels.

My heart still thumps when I recall a tiny gipsy boy, dressed in nothing but a shirt which barely reached his waist, walking along the top of a wall which dropped to a mountain gorge hundreds of feet below. Yet I am sure he was quite safe. He walked on the edge of that precipice with the assurance of a cat. I should not have

feared that a cat might fall. This child also had not yet forsaken his
guiding thread of instinct.

Here in the West we are taught to distrust our instinct from the
moment we are first squeezed into conventional patterns of behaviour. On the one hand reason, on the other brute force, usurp
the place of the invisible thread. Reason is raised up on a throne
from where it issues orders we are expected to obey. It builds an
edifice of conformity in which we all must fit. Brute force is ex-
tended till it encompasses global wars. And these two false gods of
Force and Reason are held together by a colossal will to power.

The sick and disillusioned seek again their thread. It is the task
of the analyst to help them find it. But need they ever have lost it?
I believe the small child's instinct can merge into the inner voice of
the adult without break or interruption if only we will allow it so
to do; if only we will trust our children and teach them to trust
their own sound sense instead of maintaining our prevalent over-
insistence on obedience to outer authority and conformity to the
outer pattern.

Obedience to the instinctive demands of the body is the individual's first hold on his thread from God. When I speak of the
body I am not referring particularly to sex. I refer to the behaviour of all or any part of our bodies. If we would only pay
more attention we should notice that our bodies speak to us continually.

The medical profession[2] is beginning to recognize this. It is well
known that stomach ulcers may be symptoms of anxiety and that
skin complaints are apt to have a psychological cause. Indeed our
bodies literally complain to us when we go astray. Jung has
pointed out the need to listen to this 'complaint' of any physical
symptom as well as treat it medically. If a man's throat is causing
trouble it behoves him to consider if there is some situation or
attitude he cannot swallow. If he has indigestion perhaps there is
literally something he cannot stomach.

I know one woman who from time to time is awakened in the
night by an acute pain in the rectum. Discovering on the first
occasion that it did not call for any physical action she took Jung
seriously and searched to see if she had swallowed some posionous
precept which needed to be eliminated. She was not slow to find it;
whereupon the pain immediately disappeared. She has learned

[2] See especially: A. T. W. Simeons, *Man's Presumptuous Brain*, New York,
Longmans Green.

from experience that an inadvertent over-glib psychological explanation of a happening is likely to have this painful result which
may be eliminated by emphatically throwing out the mistaken
idea.

I myself at the beginning of my analysis was worried by a pain
in the right hand when I tried to hold anything. First I could not
hold a needle, then a pen; but it was not until I could not wield a
broom without excruciating pain and I noticed that my hand was
actually swollen, that it occurred to me to tell my analyst. 'You
can't grasp things,' he suggested. Then after a moment's pause,
'Are you not failing to grasp the problems with your husband?'

I was dumbfounded. But on the way home I determined this
could not go on. If my body was refusing to function the matter
must be serious indeed. By the time I alighted from the bus the
swelling in my hand had gone and when that evening I broached
the troublesome matter with my husband I suddenly noticed that,
without thinking and without pain, I had picked up a needle and
was darning the family's socks. I have never forgotten that
lesson.

Sometimes we need to do more than allow our bodies to speak
to us, we need to allow them to act. We are taught that the body
should be the obedient servant of the mind but there are times
when servants know better than their masters. A man immersed in
books is not weak-minded because he entrusts the planting or
pruning of his roses to his gardener. And a man riding his horse
over unknown and difficult ground knows that there are times
when his horse will be a better judge than he where to put its
feet.

One's body is very like one's horse. There are occasions when
one's horse jibs at the jump because instinctively it knows that
there is hidden danger on the other side of the fence. We should
notice when our bodies jib. We should heed the situations which
make us sick in the stomach.

What we do about them is a matter for conscious decision, but
the sickness should not be ignored or treated as unimportant.
Sometimes it is helpful to notice which way our feet take us if we
leave them to choose their own direction. When neither my thinking nor my heart will tell me clearly whether I should go to a
certain place of importance, I personally notice whether I am
putting on my shoes or hanging my coat in the cupboard.

I am not for one moment suggesting that we should necessarily desist from some undertaking because we feel sick or have swollen feet, nor because obstacles sprout up on every hand. The Kontiki expedition was a marvellous example of determination overcoming every difficulty. But I am suggesting that the sickness or the obstacles should be considered as important factors in the situation and not simply ignored. Physical symptoms may tell us that we are going in the wrong direction or they may be evidence of something in the unconscious which will undermine the whole enterprise unless countered psychologically as well as with aspirin.

None the less it is the conscious mind which must make the final decisions. That is its business. When I follow the way my feet take me because I am not sure which is the right road, I am deliberately and consciously seeking the guidance of a more instinctive level of my being to help me. This is quite different from wandering about without purpose, or superstitiously following every omen.

Some horses no doubt are more reliable than others but perhaps this is because the co-operation and sympathy between rider and horse are greater. So also between a man and his body. This may be largely a question of type, and certainly of individual destiny. It may be the concern of some to dwell habitually higher up their thread than others. A philosopher is unlikely to be as in tune with his own body as a peasant. But to lose touch with it altogether is to be wholly divorced from our basic instincts and to have lost contact with an essential part of the vital thread of which I have spoken.

It is not only our bodies to which we can listen; there are other voices which will speak to us if we will only allow them to do so. We need to listen, listen all the time. Dreams also speak to those who listen with trust, and help to guide them so that they do not lose their thread.

One of the most striking instances I know of trust in the unconscious was that of a woman in England whose son was declared missing in the fighting in Africa during the last war. She was an American citizen about to be officially repatriated, but how could she leave Europe not knowing what had happened to her son? He might be in need of her. She prayed and prayed for guidance. That night she had a dream; *she was wandering uphill and down dale searching vainly for her son when suddenly she noticed that a shadowy figure was standing beside her. Then the figure spoke.*

*'Stop looking for your son,'* it said, *'he is on his way to Germany via Italy.'* She woke with this voice ringing in her ears. It was a voice of such authority that there was no room for doubt. Next day she sailed for America. Her son had in fact been taken prisoner by the Germans and he was actually taken via Italy to a prison camp in Germany, though this did not happen until two years later.

*Allow* and *trust* are the key words. We need to allow and trust the voices of the unconscious which speak to us in dreams, or through the body, while at the same time using all our faculties of thought and reason and discrimination, all our knowledge, all our strength and delicacy of feeling, all our practical good sense and the fineness of intuition with which we may be gifted. This is the paradoxical meeting of all opposites from which the Rainmaker can emerge.

If only we would learn to listen. For the most part we do not listen, we prefer to talk. We discuss, we argue, we strive to convince or we chatter about nothing at all — anything rather than listen.

I am not decrying the spoken word. Formulation in words is essential for clarity of thought, though the most subtle and the most profound truths can only be expressed indirectly in images and symbols, in poetry, in music or in colour. All art, and art is the search for truth, is the result of listening, even visual art. And truth when voiced in words is no longer talk but speech.

There is a great difference between speech and talk. Anyone can talk. It can be utterly futile or a delightful pastime. We sharpen our wits by talk and occasionally even gain a little understanding. But it is only in those rare moments when we are truly on our thread that we can speak.

Speech in a moment of inner clarity is the language of wisdom. The Rainmaker seldom even speaks. He communicates through the silence without effort and without intention.

We need to listen, and again listen, and only then to speak, or to allow the inner clarity we have attained to penetrate the silence in its own good time.

One of the most striking effects of silence which it has been my fortune to witness was that between a man and his wife.

As a girl the wife had been unusually dumb because, like so many women, she had been quite unable to put into words what she innately knew, and nothing else seemed worth talking about.

As a middle-aged woman she had an analysis and gradually learned to formulate her own inborn wisdom. Very naturally she tried to tell her intellectual husband of the inner world she was discovering, but when she put it into words she lost the essence and only succeeded in exasperating him and driving a wedge between them.

When later he became seriously ill a dream warned her that she must cease to try and get her ideas across to him. She obeyed, and during the last two weeks before he died of cancer she watched a miracle unfold before her eyes. A radiance seemed to emanate from the dying man. The house was filled with it. It affected everyone who entered. Their grown children gravitated to their father's room in a way they had never done before; and often when his wife came near his bed, he would take her hand and kiss it. One day he told her, 'I cannot tell you what you are doing for me. I never knew before all the things that were behind your mind. How should I have known? But now I know.' It was his wife's silence which enabled her to be the mediator to this dying man, not of the things in her mind, but of his own soul.

We shall do no harm, indeed we shall certainly be a force for good, by ourselves being on our own thread, but there are occasions in which we are so near to some problem concerning others that we feel we must participate.

Silence does not always seem the answer. What then can we legitimately do? Advice is generally useless. We know too little. Advice can only be given from the store of general wisdom or from our own personal experience of life.

The store of general wisdom which has crystallized into conventional attitudes frequently fails us because the particular circumstances do not fit. The commandment, 'Thou shalt not commit adultery,' if slavishly adhered to, may make us commit another sin which is, in effect, no less than murder. The moral precept or conventional advice can at times be wholly inadequate.

But neither may our personal experience of relationships and of life be wide enough to form a judgment on which we can give advice in the particular case we are considering. Moreover we do not know the pattern of another's life. Advice, even when sought, is mostly arrogance and a forgetting of the depth of our own ignorance.

Yet I believe we can do something. The first step is to disentangle ourselves and our own personal wishes from the problem and, having done so, become as conscious as possible of where we ourselves stand. Then we may provide a fixed point of reference, a post as it were stuck firmly into the sand around which a rope can be thrown from the little barques being tossed helplessly by waves of emotion. If several friends can offer firm posts, though the posts may stand for different points of view, they may yet provide some strength and stability which will help the storm-tossed people to find their own solution. Not our solution, theirs.

It is neither our advice nor our solution which is needed, but our concern. I use the word concern deliberately but perhaps I should make quite clear what I mean by it. I do not mean planning for another's welfare. I do not mean fussing over him. I do not mean nursing one's natural anxiety. And above all I do not mean exerting power in any sense whatever, physical, mental, moral or spiritual. Power is one of the most suspect of all our motives and one of the most insidious. It is so easy to exert power for someone else's good and thrive on the uplift that it gives us.

If power is the most poisonous of the false attitudes we can adopt, anxiety is the most useless. Our worry never helps anyone. It is a most destructive form of idle fantasy. We surround the person we wish to protect with a mist of anxiety which only befuddles his possibility of clear thinking or clear action. Who knows whether it may not even bring about the disasters we are trying to avoid.

To have a deep concern for anyone is to keep him in one's heart without the interference of wishing, or still worse willing, any particular goal or outcome for him; yet with faith in the purposefulness of life and the belief in the need for that individual to fulfil his own unknown destiny.

Concern is a leaving free with the utmost readiness to help if asked, and in the meantime a knowing that being on one's own thread is true tending of the soil which will provide the surest ground for the right outcome; for it will help to keep clear the channels between what is and what will be, and blow away the confusing mists between our muddled existence and the ultimate purpose of our lives.

This is to be concerned. But to know who or what claims one's concern is no easy matter. Most of us are posed with the problem nearly every day. For those whose eyes are focused on a particular piece of work, the writing of a book, the painting of a picture, the solving of a scientific problem or the attainment of a career, the matter is comparatively simple. Everything else can be swept ruthlessly aside as irrelevant, regardless of the consequent narrowing of their lives.

But those who dwell habitually on the level of diffuse awareness may find great difficulty in restricting at all the sphere of their concern. We all know those kind-hearted women who can never say no, and who dissipate their energy on people who have no real significance for them, to the detriment of those others or those matters really needing their concentration; and all without any compensating benefit to those on whom they squander themselves.

Or, on the other hand, the men who are so busy doing good works or serving a cause that they neglect their own families; and the young women who give sympathy with such warm indiscriminate readiness that they spread havoc and broken marriages around them. These latter are legion. Their intentions are not bad but they have not learned what is, and what is not, their own concern.

We know too those people who are always seeking some new experience or some new philosophy, who wander from lover to lover, or through all the ranges of psychological schools and religious sects. They also have not learned to limit themselves to their own particular concern. They seek but cannot find.

There are those who are so open to what happens around them that the chirp of every sparrow is deemed of personal significance. These are the people who have lost their personal boundaries altogether, though they are not wholly wrong, for who is to say that everything is not connected?

Most of us hover somewhere between these extremes, and every one of us has to learn how to distinguish what is, and what is not, our particular concern. The man who is pin-pointed and ruthlessly throws aside all else may be following his rightful path. Family and friends may have to stand aside while he courses through space alone. Or it may be that he has erroneously taken too narrow a path and is digging for himself a living grave, and relegating to those who love him the role of perpetual mourners.

A great Spanish philosopher[3] used to say to his students, 'Plough your furrow deep but not so deep that you cannot see over

3 Francisco Giner de los Rios.

K

the top.' For a few even that precept may not be sound. Some may
have to plough so deep that they risk losing not only width of
vision but their very lives. We cannot judge. But for most this
saying seems to be extraordinarily sound. Plough your furrow
deep but not so deep that you lose the vision of the far horizon.

What anyone's concern may be is not a question which can be
answered once for all. It changes every day. Subtly without noticing we are new each day, one day older, one day nearer death.
And if we are wise we shall notice that our concerns change too. As
we advance in years the inner demands which have rightfully lain
dormant during youth, claim our attention more and more. Or
our concern may shift from the welfare of our immediate family to
that of our particular community or group.

When the threads of two people touch, so long as they are
together that relationship is vital, no matter how inconvenient or
unconventional it may be. Threads may intertwine for a lifetime
but they do not always do so. People who cling together in obedience to nothing but convention or the law are likely, both of them,
to lose their hold on their own vital thread and find life deprived
of meaning.

Do not misunderstand me. I am not suggesting that differences
and difficulties between people should be taken as signals for separation. Suffering together may be part of the pattern, linking the
threads more firmly for all their seeming divergence. It may be an
essential prelude to new growth. Women who have had babies
will know that one must go *with* pain, not resist it, or one is torn
asunder and birth retarded. This is equally true of spiritual pain.
People leap apart to avoid their pain far too easily. So nothing
comes of it. Their renewed relationship is never born.

The acceptance of conflict and suffering is an essential part of
being on one's thread, while the deliberate search of happiness for
its own sake is, I should say, one of the best ways of ensuring that
our thread will slip from our grasp.

I have travelled full circle and return to the place from which I
started. To keep in touch with one's own vital thread is to live the
paradox of holding the opposites together, and it is this which
enables us to be concerned with others without crippling involvement, and to influence life around us without exerting power
for preconceived ends.

If we can resist the compulsive pressure of our logical thinking,
without relinquishing our precious heritage of lucid thought; if we

can hold our ground with our own hardly won ego personalities, yet bow our heads and say, 'Thy will not mine be done'; if we will but notice the reactions of our bodies; and heed the behaviour of the world towards us; if we can learn to listen to the voices within and to the whisper in the wind, with trust as well as with discrimination, we may be able to follow the road where the Rainmaker walks.

# X

# *The Older Woman*

IT WOULD SEEM easy enough for me to write on 'The Older Woman' since I am one, but perhaps it is for that very reason that I find it difficult. One can really only see situations clearly when one is outside them, not when one is in the middle of living them. However there is no help for it. When I have passed the stage of being an older woman I shall also be beyond writing at all.

It is obvious that there are two distinct classes of older women: the wife and mother on the one hand, and the professional woman on the other, although today these two merge more and more. It is with the former that I am most familiar.

The fundamental truth to remember in thinking of woman, irrespective of the role she plays, is that her life's curve, unlike that of man, is not a slow rising to the zenith of power followed by a gradual decline in the later years. The curve of a woman's life span follows more nearly the pattern of the seasons. She almost literally blossoms in the spring, but the long summer which follows is a very slow ripening with nothing much in the woman herself to show for it. If she lives a traditional family pattern she will be giving all the sap which rose so abundantly earlier to nourish her offspring, materially, emotionally and spiritually.

Then suddenly her children are all grown up, gone on their separate journeys, and she finds herself bereft. The apparent purpose of her life, for which she had strained every nerve, is snatched from her with the attainment of the goal. She feels stranded on the mud flats, while the river races by bearing away each new craft as it embarks, and she no part of the flowing waters. What then? What can happen then, with another thirty or forty years still to run and no one needing her? Even her husband has centred his life on his career and other interests apart from her while she was occupied with the growing family. At the best his need of her is not absorbing enough to assuage her aching emptiness.

What then? This is the crucial moment in the life of any wife and mother. It is then that she may notice, almost by accident, that from where the early blossoms fell fruit is hanging almost ripe. Unsuspected fruit, fruit which has swelled and grown unheeded, is now ready and waiting to be plucked. The autumn of a woman's life is far richer than the spring if only she becomes aware in time, and harvests the ripening fruit before it falls and rots and is trampled underfoot. The winter which follows is not barren if the harvest has been stored, and the withdrawal of sap is only a prelude to a new spring elsewhere.

Conscious modern women of course know these things. They prepare for the autumn before the long dry summer is over. But far too many women still feel that life is finished at fifty and that vibrant loving ends with the menopause. This last bogie should be swept away at the outset. It is utterly untrue.

You may know some version of the famous story of the young man who asked his mother at what age women cease to be interested in sexual intercourse. 'I do not know,' she replied, 'you had better ask your grandmother.' He sought out grandmother and repeated his question. 'How should I know?' she answered gruffly. 'Great Granny may be able to tell you.' This is perhaps not as far-fetched as would appear.

It is true enough that some men cease to be interested sexually in women when their physical fertility is ended, causing their wives, who have a recrudescence of sexual interest at this time, great distress. Such a situation is the survival of an inherent primitive pattern where sexuality was for humanity, as it is for animals, only a matter of procreation.

Since the age of chivalry and the development of romantic love, sex has become very much more than that. And with the discovery and spread of contraceptives sex has entered a new phase. The contraceptive can certainly lead to irresponsibility, licence and a devaluation of sexuality. In fact it often does so. But on the other hand it opens the door to immensely heightened emotional experience where sex ceases to be solely a biological function, and becomes an expression of love in its own right. In this context age with its absence of fertility is irrelevant.

This cultural achievement gives mankind a chance of healing the cleavage between body and spirit which has been fostered for centuries by the Church, and may enable us to weld once more the two together.

In this whole development the older woman is actually at a great advantage. She does not need the contraceptive, and I believe this is one reason why a woman's most profound and meaningful sex life often occurs after fifty when she is no longer caught in the biological net. For the first time she is able to give herself in the sex act completely free from fear of conception, a fear which in countless women does still operate beneath the surface, even when reason and science assure them that they have taken the most complete precautions.

Moreover to a great many women contraceptives, though accepted intellectually, are still unaesthetic, and to a deep basic feminine morality they are wholly unacceptable, all of which inevitably causes inhibitions so long as they have to be used. When once a woman is free to use her body as an expression of deep feeling, without its becoming the impersonal vehicle of nature's insistent demand for life and yet more life, she can transcend her earlier inhibitions and attain physical expression of an emotional relationship beyond anything of which she had ever dreamed.

Do not misunderstand me. It is a grave mistake for a woman to look for some great spiritual experience in sex at any age, or even to assume that she ought to have such a thing. All assumptions about sex are disastrous. They tend to lead to disappointment and recriminations. To my mind most modern books on sex do more harm than good for this very reason: they fill women's heads with assumptions and expectations which actually *prevent* experience at its fullest. It is one's own personal experience that counts and it should not be measured up against any generalization. The statistical so-called normal man or woman does not in fact exist, and it is foolish to weigh our actual living experience against such a mythical figure.

Sex delight is like happiness. It does not come when sought. It is not until a woman ceases to strive for her own sensual satisfaction, but allows the voice of her heart to speak to her man through the medium of her body, that she finds that heart, spirit and body are all one.

Important as the heightening fulfilment of sex may be, it is none the less only a small part of the ripe autumnal fruit to which I have alluded. A woman's liberation from the service of nature's purposes frees an enormous amount of energy for something else. A man at fifty is probably at the height of his intellectual or administrative power. A family woman at the same age may be aware of an entirely new stirring. Latent possibilities dance before her unbelieving eyes.

I recall one such woman seated on the lawn of her house one summer evening holding forth to her family. I say holding forth but she was certainly not laying down the law. It was almost as though a dam had burst and a torrent of ideas came tumbling out to which she herself seemed to be listening with the same astonished amusement as were her hearers. She simply emanated vitality and I remember her ending up with the words: 'I have no idea what is going to happen but I am quite sure something is.' And as I watched and listened so was I. She did in fact become a writer some ten years later.

The expression 'change of life' exactly fits the situation. The menopause does not spell the end of life but a change of direction, not a living death but a change of *life*.

If this were more generally understood I am convinced that women's menopause problems would rapidly diminish. Glandular changes are inevitable but it is woman's own dread of this mysterious change on the whole tenor of her life which, I am sure, brings about the neurotic state she fears. No, change of life means an enormous release of energy for some new venture in a new direction.

The direction in which the newly released energy will flow depends of course entirely on the type of person and the particular gifts with which she has been endowed. Some may develop a latent talent, painting, writing or some such thing. Voluntary societies serving social, political and cultural causes of all kinds abound with such women. But these only cater for the more conscious and extraverted type of woman. There are innumerable others who can find no outlet. They suffer deeply, for energy which finds no channel in which to flow seeps into the ground and makes a marsh where nothing can be planted, where only slime and insects breed.

Women who find they are no longer vitally needed by their families yet have no other place where they can give themselves, sink into lassitude and finally fall ill. The magnates who organize society have hardly begun to notice this happening. The autumnal energy of countless older women escapes silently down the kitchen sink along with their tears.

Not only is the nation poorer for its loss, the wastage is double, for these women who could have been healthily active and useful become a wholly unnecessary burden upon the health services, while as likely as not their frustration poisons the atmosphere of the home. Swamps breed mosquitoes. Uncanalized, wasted energy breeds gloom and nagging.

Part-time work is at least one answer to this problem, but part-time work is not easy to find. Industry seems to frown upon it and our modern passion for degrees and paper diplomas shuts many a door. It is not sufficiently recognized that running a home can afford very valuable experience in organization, and particularly in handling other people with diverse temperaments. The mother of a family is generally an adept at that very difficult accomplishment of attending to half a dozen things all at the same time, an asset by no means to be despised if diverted to other fields.

That society is gravely at fault in not providing outlets for the older woman's energy is unquestionably true. But her real problem is to discover in which direction her newly released libido wants to flow. Libido is like water, it always seeks its proper level. No amount of coercion can make it flow uphill.

So long as a woman is fulfilling her traditional role of bringing up a family, she is carried along by the stream of life. Indeed she has no alternative. She goes with the stream even though cooking and cleaning and changing diapers are not at all her ideal occupations. She has no real choice. But she herself develops as the family grows and she learns to meet the demands as they arise. Changing diapers gives way to helping with obstreperous homework and providing meals for expanding appetites in every field. But when all this is past and the river flows on without her, her own little stream of energy is dammed up. If she is fortunate the waters will rise till they are strong enough to burst out in a channel of their own.

What the channel will be depends on her concern. Even today, when education does its best to divert women's activity into every branch of industry and money-making, there are still older women who slide happily into the estate of grandmother because their children's children do in fact become the centre of their interest and their concern. Dedicated grandmothers who gladly put themselves at the service of the future generation without trying to run the show themselves are a boon to any family, but they are becoming increasingly rare. Like maiden aunts they are dying out, and the services which both maiden aunts and grandmothers used to give as a matter of course and with genuine devotion now frequently have to be bought with money. We all know what a poor substitute that is and how expensive.

The modern trend seems to be in the opposite direction. More and more mothers wait with impatience for their children to be grown and gone. Then at last they feel free to carry on with the career which family demands had forced them to abandon. These women are faced with relatively little conflict. They nearly always succeed in finding an outlet before the problem becomes acute. As the children grow they dovetail the new life into the old so that there is no traumatic moment when they feel deserted.

The ones who cannot look forward to any vibrant future or any sphere of usefulness to which they can give themselves, are those with whom I am particularly concerned here. For them especially is the surprise and delight of discovery. And for them above all is the paramount need to know what is and what is not their true concern.

I spoke about concern in my previous chapter on the Rainmaker. I will not repeat what I said then. But in the case of woman, the outstanding almost invariable object of her concern is, as we all know, the person or persons whom she loves. This is true right through her life. It is, I repeat, the essential ingredient of her nature. When she is true to herself love is her primal driving force. Love and the service of those she loves. I mean a wholly personal love, not the love of causes or of country. I believe this to be true for all the various ranks of women, and it is as true of professional women as of wives and mothers. It is not always apparent that this is so. We are all very good at covering up our mainspring. But I have yet to meet the woman who did not know in her heart that love is her main concern and that the secret of her success in any field was her personal love in the background.

Men really can give themselves to a cause, working wholeheartedly for it and inspired by it. Unless their ingredient of masculinity is very great, women cannot. If one is allowed to penetrate their secrets one finds beneath their apparent impersonal enthusiasms some very personal love, the existence of which makes them feel whole and gives them the energy which enables them to act.

The schoolgirl will work double for a teacher whom she loves. The career woman will either have a person who is the focus of her love at work who provides her dynamism, or some love outside which is her stimulus. It may be a lover in the background or children for whom she needs to earn.

Wherever I look I meet this incontrovertible fact that a woman always needs some person to do things *for*, even though to the outsider there is no apparent connection with the loved person and what she may be doing. We all know how difficult it is for a woman even to cook a meal for herself. She cannot be bothered. A bit of bread and cheese will do. But if there is someone to cook *for* she prepares quite elaborate dishes with delight.

The same prevails throughout. The work of a woman, whether factory hand or professional, will be quite different in quality if in some way she can connect it with her love. I have talked with women artists, painters, singers, actors. They all agree that art in itself is seldom quite enough. Beneath their devotion to their art is some person whom they love and for whom in some mysterious inner way they perfect their art. Even the nun, who is an extreme case of selfless devotion, is contained in and inspired by a very personal love of Christ. I suspect that men are far more single-mindedly purposeful.

The need to have someone to do things for comes out in most curious places. I recall a woman who was threatened with blindness which only an operation could prevent. Operations of any kind had always been anathema to her, and the thought of an eye operation was more than she could face. She raged internally at the meddlesomeness of doctors. Why couldn't she be allowed to go blind in peace? Then suddenly she realized what she might be doing to her children and grandchildren if she went blind. A blind old grandmother was the last thing she wanted to impose on them. Her torment ceased. She entered hospital without a further qualm. She had found someone to have her operation *for*.

This tendency only to be able to do things for someone whom one loves makes it difficult for a woman to know what she herself really wants. She is often accused quite naturally by men of futility or hypocrisy, because when asked what she wants to do, she replies 'Whatever you like.' But it is not hypocrisy. She really means that her desire is to to do what he wants. It has not occurred to her to have any special preference. Even if she knew she wanted to dance it would give her no pleasure to do so if her lover was longing to watch a cricket match. This adaptability is not unselfishness and has no particular merit. It is the way a woman functions. Perhaps I am describing the last generation. I think it possible that the present generation of women not only know themselves better but are far more decisive than the last, thus changing their relationship with men. Whether the change is for the good, or rather a disaster, is still an open question. Perhaps it is both.

However this may be, the older woman's dilemma is precisely here. If no one whom she loves wants her services there is no one to do things for. There is in fact no reason for which to live. She is faced with an entirely new situation in which for the first time maybe she has to discover what are her *own* wishes, her *own* tastes and in which direction her energy, with no love focus to act as magnet, will consent to flow. It is fascinating to notice how a widow will sometimes reverse the habits of a married lifetime after her husband's death. The extent to which she does so is the measure of her earlier adaptability.

In the following poem I have tried to express an old woman's bewilderment. It is called 'The Last Years':

Now that my loves are dead
On what shall my action ride?

I will not make my children
Lovers nor tune my time
By footsteps of the young
To ease my solitude;

But sing of springs, forgotten
In slow summer's tedium,
And autumn ripe with fruit;
Of winter branches, bare

Beneath the storm, bowed
With weight of rain, and after,
Lifting knotted fingers
Towards a translucent sky;

And wrest from the gathered sheaf
Forgiveness, buried in the heart
Of every grain, to knead
My bread for sustenance.

My action, sharing bread,
Love becomes ability
To bless, and be, in blessing,
Blessed.

To go back and collect up one's past as this poem suggests, writing it down in poems or as good prose as one can achieve, has in itself a healing effect. I believe one has to return to one's past, not once but many times, in order to pick up all the threads one has let fall through carelessness or unobservance.

I believe above all one has to return again and again to weep the tears which are still unshed. We cannot feel all the grief of our many losses at the time we suffer them. That would be too crippling. But if we would really gather our whole lives into a single whole, no emotion that belongs to us should be left unfelt.

Moreover, the review of our lives enables us to notice the constant repetition of the same pattern of happening, met by the same pattern of behaviour. Seeing this we cannot help being struck by the apparent purposefulness of every detail of our lives even though we do not like our fate. Those who do in fact gather up and write their story are enormously enriched. And women for whom nothing is worth the effort unless it is for the sake of someone they love, can write their outer or their inner story quite deliberately for their own grandchildren (if they have any) to read when they are grown up. If there are no grandchildren, most women will need to find someone else to write it for.

What fascinating pictures of antiquated ways of living we should have if this were done more often. Every single person has the material for at least one book. It is, I think, important that publication should not be the aim. Too many books are published already. Too many mediocre pictures are put upon the market. No, the aim is creativity for its own sake. The grandchildren or some other persons are merely the excuse which the aging woman needs to enable her to make the effort.

Creativity once begun goes on. Nothing is so satisfying to the human soul as creating something new. If the old can become creative in their own right they are lost no longer. We all long to see our works in print, I know, but this is not the point. It is the act of creation which counts. Every act of creation adds to the creativity in the world, and who knows if it has not some similar effect as the ritual breathing towards the East at dawn of those primitive tribes who believe that their breath helps the sun to rise.

Unless some outer activity claims her, the family woman may make the discovery earlier than either men or professional women that libido changes its direction as old age approaches. It is a change that all must encounter sooner or later: at some time or other outer activities lose their glamour and the inner world demands attention. So strong is this demand that the old who refuse to turn their faces inwards, clinging desperately to outer values even though they watch them daily slipping from their grasp, are frequently made ill. Forced by illness or accident to be inactive, they are given the opportunity which they had been unable to take of their own free will, to ruminate and ponder and put forth new shoots in an unaccustomed inner world.

Illnesses at any time of life should not be merely cured, but utilized for growth in a hitherto unknown field. Particularly does this apply to the aging, whether man or woman.

If the old can become creative in their own right, they are, as I have said, lost no longer, but above all it is imperative that the older person should have a positive attitude towards death. The young can forget death with impunity. The old cannot. They are fortunate indeed who have faith that they will not be extinguished when they die, and can look forward to a new beginning in some other dimension or some other realm. But faith is a gift. Like love it comes by grace. No amount of thought or striving can achieve it; which paradoxically does not mean that there is no need to strive. We get from life in the measure with which we give to it, and our fundamental attitudes demand unceasing strife. But this is only preparing the soil. The actual planting of a spiritual seed like faith is beyond our control. It comes when it will.

To those who have been denied such faith I would ask, is it not a fact that the people who accept death most readily are the ones who have lived most fully? I do not mean necessarily the people who have done the most. Outer visible achievement is no criterion of living fully. The life of a great business magnate whose industry has erected huge buildings, set innumerable wheels whizzing and employs thousands of people, may have been so narrowly focused on the gain of material wealth that the riches of the spirit, art, music, literature and the warmth of human contacts, may have escaped him altogether. This is not full living.

At the opposite extreme I recall Spanish beggars seated on the cathedral steps, idly watching the passers by, receiving as though it were their lawful due occasional gifts of alms with a dignified 'God bless you'. How well the beggar must know those oft recurrent faces, nearly as constant in their daily presence as the stone saints and gargoyles behind him, the hourly chiming of the cathedral bells and the chant from within the church. What a setting in which to dwell and ponder! Does this man live fully? I do not know, but Unamuno, one of Spain's greatest writers believed he did. Unamuno even declared that the most interesting philosopher he had ever met was a beggar, one of a long line of beggars.

I am not advocating beggary, but neither it nor visible achievement is any criterion of the quality of living. There is no yardstick for the surmounting of obstacles, the wrestling with angels and the transcending of suffering.

There is no yardstick for the measurement of others, but maybe for ourselves there is. One's yardstick is one's full capacity to *be* as complete a person as within one lies, and that includes becoming as conscious as it is possible for one to be in order to bring out and develop the buried talents with which one was born, and in order to realize one's own innate knowledge.

The more diverse the talents of any person, the more difficult may be the task. We only have a certain amount of psychic energy and throughout our lives we have to choose the road we will take, abandoning the fascinating paths in other directions. But the development of an ability to choose, and the consistent following of the path chosen, may be a large part of becoming as whole a person as one can be. So also is our flexibility a very real asset. The man or woman who has chosen the wrong path by mistake, and we all make mistakes, may need to retrace his steps and start again. This needs courage and should not be mistaken for the idle whim of the dilettante. Moreover, many people follow a vital thread towards a wholly invisible goal. We cannot possibly judge the value of their achievement.

To be conscious is not in itself a goal. It is possible to be a highly conscious person without one's character being influenced at all. Consciousness is not enough in itself. But one cannot develop a gift if one does not know that it is there, so to be conscious is indispensable. Many of us, through ignorance of our own capacities, only allow a small part of ourselves to flower. Neither can one lop off a branch that is marring the beauty of a tree if one has not noticed its presence and seen that its unbridled growth is spoiling the harmony of the whole. Or it may have to be sacrificed because it is impeding the growth of other plants.

Our individual psyche is very like a garden. The kind of garden will be determined by the nature of the soil, whether it is on a mountain slope or in a fertile valley. It will depend upon the climate. Green lawns flourish in England. In parts of Spain to sow

a lawn is to make a present to the wind, for literally the seed is
blown away.

Climate and geology are powers beyond our altering. They are
the conditions we have been given to make the most of it, and for
some the task is immensely harder than it is for others. The slopes
of arid hills in Spain are a marvel of man's endeavour. Every inch
is terraced with little walls of stones so that not a drop of the rare
precious rain shall be lost in tumbling streams but held for the
thirsty vines and olive trees. All honour to such gardeners. Some of
us dwell in more temperate climes where the task is not so hard,
but any gardener will know the unceasing vigilance which is
needed to tend a garden, wherever it may be. Weeds are never
eradicated once for all.

So, too, our psyches. They also can be invaded by pests from
other gardens which have been neglected, making it harder to
maintain the health of ours. Indeed, to maintain our psyche or our
garden free of pests is a responsibility to our neighbours as well as
to ourselves. Some gardens are more formal than others. Some
have corners deliberately left wild, but a garden with no form and
no order is not a garden at all but a wilderness.

The psyche which is a total wilderness ends in the asylum or
burdens its family with unhealthy emanations. The well-tended
but over conventional garden, on the other hand, may have no
stamp of individuality upon it. It expresses the psyche of the mass
man, and suburbia is full of them. The garden which is tended
with care yet is not quite like any other garden, for it conveys the
atmosphere of its owner, is like the psyche of an individual who
has become a mature personality from where the scent of honey-
suckle and roses and wild thyme will perfume the air for all around.

But gardens cannot grow without earth, and the loveliest
flowers thrive on soil that is well manured and black. Dirt has been
defined as matter in the wrong place. Manure is not dirt when dug
into the borders. And rich emotional living in the right places is as
indispensable for the flowering of wisdom in old age as the purity
of the air and the brilliant sunlight of consciousness. No flower and
no wisdom was ever reared on a ground of shiny white tiles washed
daily with antiseptic.

It is the older person, whether man or woman, who has the
need and the obligation to tend the garden of the psyche. The
young are generally too immersed in active living; study, work,
careers, and bringing up a family absorb all their energies. Indeed,

a too early absorption with their own psyche may be an actual poison for the young. It may deprive them of the essential spontaneity which is needed for living. Actual experience can never be replaced by thinking about life or examining inner motives. To be ever conscious of the possible hazards before us snatches away our power to leap. We can only live fully by risking our lives over and over again.

It is in the latter part of life that people need to turn attention inwards. They need to do so because if their garden is as it should be they can die content, feeling that they have fulfilled their task of becoming the person they were born to be. But it is also an obligation to society. What a man or woman is within affects all those around. The old who are frustrated and resentful because they have omitted to become in life the persons they should have been, cause all in their vicinity to suffer.

Being is not the same as doing. Most people have had to sacrifice in some direction their capacity to *do*, but none are exempt from *being* to the full. There can be no limit to one's endeavour to become more and more aware of the depths of one's own psyche, discovering its lights and its shadows, its possibilities of unexpected vision as well as its dark regions.

The old woman, like the old man, needs to turn her natural receptivity towards the inner voices and inner whisperings, pondering on the new ideas which will come to her if she is attuned to her own inner self. Mrs. Moore, in E. M. Forster's *Passage to India*, was doing precisely this in her sudden and unexpected refusal to be drawn into the whirl of outer events. But we should not expect the insights of the *very* old to be revealed to the rest of us. There may be weeks and months or even years of slow, quiet gestation in the minds of quite old people. To speak of half-formed ideas is to destroy their growth as surely as to burn a seedling with the sun's rays shining through a magnifying glass. The very frailty of age guards its secrets.

Indeed, the insights of the very old may never quite reach the level of consciousness where they can be clothed in words. But this does not mean that they are not at work beneath the surface. The conscious mind is only a small part of our total psyche.

The very old, those who have given up all interest in the outer world even to the stage of being withdrawn from any point of contact, may still be receiving and quietly nurturing within themselves new insights which will enable them to meet the unknown future. One wonders sometimes what holds them here. Perhaps they are not ready. They cannot die till they are ready. I have often felt that modern medicine is very cruel to the old for it keeps them here when they are longing to be allowed to go.

But perhaps longing to go is not the same as being ready to meet the other side. I doubt if science could keep anyone alive if in this sense they were truly ready for their death.

It is a fallacy that the old are necessarily lonely when they are alone. Some are. But never those who are quietly pondering, preparing themselves, albeit without deliberate intention, for their coming death. They need long hours of solitude to round out their lives within, as they have earlier done without.

There is a lovely little book *All Passion Spent*, by Victoria Sackville-West. She tells of an old lady after the death of her husband with whom she has shared a long life. Her children hold a family council. What can be done with mother? They plan it all out. She shall stay with them and their growing families in turn so they can share the burden of looking after her and keeping her from feeling lonely.

The plan is unfolded to the old lady who, to the amazement of her children, thanks them politely and declines their offer of hospitality. It transpires that for years she has been longing to have a little house of her own where she could live alone and undisturbed with her thoughts. Miraculously the chance had come and nothing should cheat her of it now.

This old woman had the good fortune to know her own mind, which many of us do not. Many old men and women are cheated of their essential solitude, and kept continually focused on outer things by the mistaken kindness of the young and their own unawareness of their need to be alone. We die alone. It is well to become accustomed to being alone before that moment comes.

Old age is the time of reckoning, our achievements balanced by our needless omissions and our mistakes. Some of our mistakes are hideous, but this is no reason for not facing them. Some we would never know if our children did not tell us the awful things we had done to them without realizing the dire effect of our advice, the example of our behaviour or our condemnation.

The old are generally too much shielded. The next generation fears to hurt them. I say the next generation deliberately for it is seldom the young who overshield the old. The vital calls to live of the young are more likely to make them callous, which is really far more healthy. It is those who are already advanced in middle age, often themselves already older women, who over-protect the very old. Nothing must be told to worry them. They must have every comfort and never be left. Frequently they are so pampered and humoured that they are turned into querulous children.

Indeed, it is more often than not our own dislike of feeling hard, rather than genuine affection, which makes us so falsely kind. Moreover there is no need for us to take upon ourselves the responsibility of sheltering the very old from worry. Griefs do not shatter them as they do the young. They have their own protection from those emotions which are more than they can bear. It is not our task to turn them into breathing fossils.

That is no kindness to the old. Rather it is cruelty because it deprives them of their power still to grow. It is an unpardonable belittling of the role of the aged, for it is they who, whether they can formulate it or not, are in fact the depositories of wisdom. Very often it is they who have lived more than those who shelter them. To the older woman who has the aged in her care I would say: Be careful not to spend more energy upon the very old than you can rightly afford to do. Your own life too makes claims. Deep thought and wise judgment are needed to give them libido where it is really due. If too much is given to the aged at the expense of the giver it will only breed bitterness, and that helps no one.

The care of the very old is a terribly difficult problem and every case has to be dealt with on its own merits. Many family women find an old parent a good substitute for the children who have grown and gone. Many others who have had no children turn the parent unwittingly into the child they have never had. In either case the old person is wrapped in cotton wool which he or she has not the strength to throw aside. They can very easily become victims, rather than grateful recipients, of our over-coddling.

And so they end their days either with a complacency to which they have no right, or in puzzled resentment that the young do not give them the love they thought they had deserved. There are no deserts in love. Greater outspokenness is better for everyone concerned, though the young might certainly temper their frankness with the constant remembrance that the old have done their best. Deliberate malice on the part of parents is, I believe, very rare. The vast majority of parents undoubtedly do the best they know. And as undoubtedly the next generation will have found it wrong, and rightly so. To be a parent is the most difficult task in the world. For a parent not to be understanding enough cripples. To be too understanding imprisons.

I have yet to meet the parents who have not made serious blunders with their children in one direction or the other. The childless in this are fortunate. The false steps they have taken in life are likely to have had less dire consequences on others.

I think it is important that mistakes should be brought out into the light of day, for how otherwise may they be forgiven? Forgiven by those sinned against but also forgiven by the sinner himself. This is something very different from complacency for it implies full consciousness and condemnation of the sin. To forgive oneself is a very difficult thing to do, but perhaps it is the last task demanded of us before we die. For the man or woman who can forgive him- or herself can surely harbour no vestige of rancour against any other.

Impersonal forgiveness is very like love, but love on a higher plane than the personal love which women above all find so necessary. It is Agape as distinct from personal Eros. It is the charity spoken of by St. Paul. It is only possible for those who are completely on their own thread to God. No little isolated ego can forgive itself. In the last verses of the poem quoted the old woman found forgiveness of herself as well as others to be her inspiration and her goal.

And so, in the end, if endeavour is unceasing and the fates are kind, almost without noticing how it happened an old woman may find that love is still, as it always had been, the centre and the mainspring of her being, although, along with her years, the word has grown in meaning.

# XI

# Soul Images of Woman[1]

I OFFERED TO write this paper in a rash moment. I have found it much more difficult to do than I had anticipated. The occasion which spurred me to make the effort was Dr. R. D. Scott's lecture on schizophrenic women patients, in the course of which he said, 'It is as though they had no anima.' During the discussion it was queried whether women could in fact have an anima, as the concept of anima referred to man's psychology, to which Dr. Scott replied that he had not known what else to call it. I suggested that 'soul' was perhaps the word he was looking for and to this he acquiesced.

There was undoubtedly confusion in all our minds, for as someone said, why not call it animus? I felt the time had come to try to clarify, hence this paper.

It is common knowledge that the unconscious of man is feminine and that the anima in some form or other is its personification. And it is generally accepted that the personification of the unconscious of woman is the animus. So long as the unconscious is considered as a whole that is good enough, but with greater differentiation of the images of the unconscious it becomes clear that the pattern of woman's psyche is not just that of man the other way round. At the very beginning of her life she emerges from a feminine being, like herself, which no man does, and this in itself must make a great difference in attitude.

With analysis man becomes aware of other figures, masculine shadows of all kinds, a wise old man, etc., but the figure of the anima which seems to represent his innermost soul always remains feminine.

This paper is asking a question: As women become aware of the other figures of the unconscious, feminine shadows etc., do their innermost souls continue to be represented by a male figure or not?

---

[1] This lecture—keystone of the author's thoughts—was found among her papers.

Many women are troubled with the idea that they do and I personally believe that they do not.

I am, however, convinced that a woman cannot find her feminine soul image at all unless she first becomes on very good terms with her animus. It is he in fact who, bearing aloft his torch, leads the way into the innermost recess where the soul image of a woman so successfully hides. As it is he whom a woman meets first he may appear to be himself the soul image she is seeking; but if she ventures with him further into the dark and unknown she may find that he does not himself represent her soul but is rather acting as her guide towards it.

In this context the dreams sometimes speak of the animus as the father of a woman's soul image. Several dreams have come my way which seem to bear out the idea that the animus is not himself the image of a woman's soul, but the father of that image. And though to do so is to forestall my argument I should like to give you one of these dreams straight away in order to make it clearer what I am trying to get at in this talk.

This was the dream of a woman a little over fifty who had had considerable analysis, and who had years earlier recognized and digested the implications of her own incestuous daughter-father relationship in the unconscious. She described this dream as one of the most exciting dreams she had ever had. I will give it to you in her own words: *I was going up the stairs of a humble house accompanied by a little girl aged twelve with loose hair who looked exactly like the early photos of myself. In the top room we knew we should find this child's father. Who could he be? I had no idea. Suspense mounted at every step until we reached the attic door. I knocked and slowly opened it. To my utter astonishment in the middle of a bare room I saw a man kneeling on the floor in an attitude of prayer. He was the well-known inner figure with whom I habitually conversed when doing active imagination, and whom I had come to regard as my own creative animus.*

So here this woman's most advanced, co-operative, creative animus was described as the father of this little pre-adolescent girl. If she had been a small boy I should not have been surprised. It would have seemed natural enough that this animus figure should father a male child, standing perhaps for the whole enterprise of becoming conscious. Yet it was inconceivable that with such a father this particular little girl could be the dreamer's infantility. I am aware that the Self will sometimes appear in the form of a child but I cannot imagine that an animus could ever be styled the father of the Self. What else then could this little girl be but the dreamer's own soul image before it got overlaid with a masculine education and hidden out of sight? And this idea immediately brought numbers of other dreams to mind where this same child had appeared before without adequate explanation. If she were a soul image then they all fitted into a pattern, in particular a very early hitherto inexplicable dream where she had appeared up against the wall some feet from the ground like a shadowy bas-relief with arms outstretched making her falling draperies look like wings.

Once conscious of who she was this figure grew up and now appears an ageless but very feminine woman. She no longer resembles the dreamer for she, though not this soul child, has adopted a persona with which to meet the world. But if ever the dreamer deliberately calls her to mind she appears accompanied by another figure who is undoubtedly an image of the Self. If on the other hand in moments of extremity she appeals to the Self, this latter will appear holding the soul image by the hand.

I will presently give you some more dreams, my own and other women's, but if you will allow me I want to go back and consider what we mean by certain psychological concepts which we so blithely bandy about, and try to explain in what sense I am using them. I have to confess that I am not at all clear myself and I am only trying to place before you my own very tentative way of seeing things.

Perhaps you will bear with me if I ask you for a moment to follow the course of my own muddled thinking, not because my particular muddle is valuable but because the elucidation of some-one else's confusion sometimes helps to clarify one's own, and I am sure that many of you are quite as muddled as I am.

The concept of animus was my first big puzzle. I have for a long time been trying to understand it, in fact I once wrote a paper on the animus to rid myself of the uneasy suspicion, shared by many women, that to have an animus problem was a polite way of saying one was smitten by the plague.

At that time it seemed to me that all attempts by a woman to focus or analyse were carried out with the help of her animus. It was her animus which studied or embarked on a career. It was her animus which enabled her to analyse and discriminate, her animus which brought to her notice all the well-worn truths which culture had formulated. This figure it seemed to me was positive and helpful so long as the woman took the precaution of informing him how she, as woman, felt about the matters in hand and only became negative when she failed to do so. For then, being deprived of the essential data of her feeling he had no alternative but to voice the general truths of the day. These, through her own omission with regard to her feelings, turn out to be no more than clichés, irrelevant to the actual situation. Irrelevance is, I believe, as I have said elsewhere, the invariable signature tune of a negative animus statement.

That was how I saw the animus: as the total focusing power of a woman whether she was focusing on the outer or the inner world. But on the other hand I realized that women are also driven by an immensely strong life force, sometimes going with it in accordance with their nature, but quite often unwilling victims, compelled along a course or plunged into entanglements which they do not want but are quite unable to resist.

It was only gradually that I realized that my picture of women driven by the life force on the one hand, and on the other focusing and discriminating solely with the good offices of the animus, itself a collective figure, had left no place for an ego at all.

I got out of my difficulty by deciding that for a woman at least the ego was only the chooser, that part of her which could say to the impersonal forces impinging upon her, 'Yes, all right I will go that way,' or, 'No, no, I refuse to be driven there, or accept this, that or the other slogan.'

This seemed all right for a while though I still felt that a woman's ego, according to me, was having a very thin time, which did not seem to fit at all the young women with whom I talked, many of whom had no doubt that they were the possessors of strong, reliable egos of far more substance than my 'chooser'.

It was with something of a shock that I realized one day that the thing I called 'I' was not by any means the chooser but something far deeper and more elusive. I saw that I was actually identifying in my own mind far more with a figure which had already appeared again and again in dreams, the figure of a woman whom I had learned was never far away from the image of the Self yet always distinguishable from it, a figure I had learned to think of as an image of the soul.

Though my animus warned me that to identify with the soul seemed dangerously like an inflation, the idea refused to leave me.

I began to notice that women really were identified with their souls. The idea was not new. I had heard it before. I recall Philip Metman saying, 'Woman *is* soul.' Mrs. Jung had said it and so had Barbara Hannah, but I was understanding this statement for the first time.

Gradually I realized that there was nothing inflated about it. Everyone is born with a soul. But women, being closely tied to their original instinctive pattern, are less easily separated from their essential soul by the development of intellect and so continue to identify with it. You will remember Eva Metman's contention that little girls remain in contact with the Self in the way that a boy does not. This is another way of saying the same thing. To identify with the Self is an inflation indeed. But to recognize that one is a soul inhabiting a body is to know who one is. And this comes more easily to women than to men.

What my ego could be was still a mystery, but I was convinced that the thing which used my tongue to communicate with the world outside, or the world within, and was continually saying 'I', could with impunity stand up against and refute at any particular moment the dictates of the animus, but it belied the soul at its peril. To do that was an utter betrayal of one's essential being. I was forced to the conclusion that the soul is the essential core and the ego merely its mouthpiece. This does not remove from the ego the role of chooser. It can choose *not* to be the mouthpiece of the soul. It can choose *not* to go with the Self or it can choose consciously to do so of its own freewill.

Still bewildered, Neumann came to the rescue. In his *Origins of Consciousness* he depicts the emergence of the masculine ego from the feminine matrix of the unconscious. And in his essay entitled 'On the Moon and Matriarchal Consciousness' published in *Spring*, 1954,[2] he put forward the idea that the focused consciousness of the ego is always masculine whether in man or woman, but that there is another layer of more diffuse awareness which is feminine in character even when found in man, this awareness not to be confused with the unconscious itself.

I hailed this with relief. In my own thinking I had given far too much to the animus, thus largely denuding woman of a conscious ego. Neumann redressed the situation. His conception of a masculine ego in both sexes conceded to women the ability to analyse and discriminate in their own right without having to call on a

[2] *Spring*, Analytical Psychology Club of New York.

conceptual archetype to help them. In talking to modern women this seems wholly acceptable. My notion that they were only intelligent people by virtue of an animus had grated uneasily.

If Neumann is right that the ego is masculine in women as well as in men, it would not be very surprising to find that the soul appears as a feminine figure not only in men but also in women.

For years I have been collecting dreams which show how women themselves visualize their souls, but first of all, what do I mean by that word 'soul'?

Naturally I turned to Jung. Perhaps English-speaking people who do not know German and are dependent on translations are unduly confused because the English word soul and the German word *seele* do not mean the same thing. Whether anima and soul mean the same thing is continually a puzzle to many people, still worse soul and animus.

In *Psychological Types*, after a long description of the anima, Jung says, 'If, therefore, we speak of the *anima* of a man we must logically speak of the *animus* of a woman, if we are to give the soul of woman its right name.'[3] That was written more than thirty years ago. This sentence has caused great trouble to innumerable women to whom it does not ring true. Mrs. Jung was one of the first to point out that to many women's ears it did not click. I have been at pains to search Dr. Jung's more recent writings to see whether or not he still retains his early definition of a woman's soul. I was relieved to find that neither in *Aion* nor in *The Archetypes and the Collective Unconscious*, nor in the revised edition of *Two Essays on Analytical Psychology* is there a single suggestion that the animus is the equivalent of a woman's soul.

In *Aion* he explicitly states that he is not using the word soul at all but prefers the term anima as indicating something specific. The animus is portrayed as woman's representative of the Eternal Logos. He is the word, the power to formulate, to analyse, to discriminate between the opposites. This is nowhere equated with soul.

The animus is indeed woman's faculty to separate, not unite; which is why, if she is trying to make a relationship as a woman, she had better keep this analytical separating part of her well out of the situation or he will wreck it with his impersonal, collective character.

3 C. G. Jung, *Collected Works*, Vol. 6, Par. 805, Princeton University Press.

In *Aion* Jung describes the positive aspect of the animus in these
words:

> Through the figure of father he expresses not only conven-
> tional opinions but — equally — what we may call 'spirit',
> philosophical or religious ideas in particular, or rather the
> attitude resulting from them. Thus the animus is a psycho-
> pomp, a mediator between the conscious and the unconscious
> and a personification of the latter. Just as the anima becomes,
> through integration, the Eros of consciousness, so the animus
> becomes a Logos; and in the same way that the anima gives
> relationship and relatedness to a man's consciousness, the ani-
> mus gives to woman's consciousness a capacity for reflection,
> deliberation, and self-knowledge.[4]

Here the animus is explicitly described, not as soul but as spirit
or meaning, and I do not think any woman will quarrel with that;
but the question still remains what does she mean by a soul and
what do I mean in this paper? I am certainly not thinking of the
attitude resulting from philosophical or religious ideas, nor the
function of relationships which Jung has elsewhere called the
anima. Nor have I found that Victor White's *Soul and Psyche*
helps me.

It was not until I turned to the language of poets that I was able
to get myself at all clear. The soul has always been referred to as
immortal and poets have invariably spoken of the eyes as the
windows of the soul. The soul looks out through the eyes and we
penetrate their depths in search of another soul.

The eyes of Dr. Scott's schizophrenic patients were vacant. No
soul looked out. These women were alive and functioning more or
less, possessed perhaps by some partial aspect of themselves or at
the mercy of an archetype, but no personal soul looked out of their
eyes for they had lost contact with their souls and were wandering
in chaos.

May I repeat here an image I have used earlier: in my way of
envisaging life I see everyone of us as being linked to God by an
invisible thread. The lowest point is his body and the thread passes
up through heart and head and spiritual aspirations. The angels
or images of the Self which it is vouchsafed to anyone to see are I
believe only those which embrace his particular thread. I mean

[4] *Ibid*, Vol. 9, ii, Par. 33.

embrace for such a figure may embrace or hold more than one person's thread. These are the intermediaries between him and God, and somewhere in their vicinity and yet always inseparable from them dwells I believe the individual's immortal soul which looks out of a man's or woman's eyes in a way with which we are all familiar.

To be on one's thread is to be in touch with the Self so that life has meaning. It is when we lose touch with our vital thread that we feel lost, forsaken, and life purposeless. This can happen to any of us on occasions in varying degrees but the schizophrenic has for the time being let go of his thread altogether. His soul cannot find the windows through which to look out. They are shuttered up or blocked by an invader.

In this talk I am trying to limit the use of the word soul to its popular usage in the English language as the essential and immortal part of any person, from the moment he is born. It is this immortal essence that looks out of a baby's eyes the moment it can see and smile. It movingly greets one from the eyes of any small child before it has learned to conceal itself from the world's intruding gaze. May I, in parenthesis, add that I am begging no question here in taking for granted the immortality of the soul. It is a question I am not asking. Man has always taken it for granted and Jung in his B.B.C. television interview declared, not his belief, but his knowledge that the soul survives; for man, as he said in his closing words, cannot lead a meaningless existence. Moreover, I am not the only person who feels that they know from their own experience that the soul continues after death.

The purpose of this paper is not inquiry into the immortality of the soul but into how women actually envisage their immortal souls in the hierarchy of images with which the unconscious presents them.

As I have already said, at the outset the whole of the unconscious of a man is projected upon a woman, notably his mother, and it is only gradually that he comes to recognize masculine figures whether of the wise old man or devilish shadows. But the image of woman continues to hold for him his own soul qualities in the person of the anima, whether or not he projects the figure on to an actual woman. With a woman on the other hand, though the first total projection of the unconscious may indeed be on to a man, with greater differentiation I hope to show that with some women at least the soul image appears as a feminine figure. I think this may have some bearing on the well-known fact that whereas women generally carry a man's anima projection gladly and without strain, only revolting when the image projected is confused with a lot of extraneous characteristics, such as for instance qualities which belong to the man's mother, men do not seem to carry a woman's animus projection so readily. He is often irked and irritated by it. I find it hard to believe that a man objects to being the bearer of an image of Logos, the giver of meaning. To carry this is his legitimate pride. Experience also seems to show his readiness to play the role of authority and capability. But it occurs to me that the real reason for his exasperation may be that the woman, in addition to projecting her animus on to him where it may legitimately dwell, frequently looks to him also to reflect for her her soul, and this he cannot do for the simple reason that he is not sufficiently identified with his own soul to be able to mirror that of another.

A woman may indeed carry his soul for him until he can take it into himself, for the nebulous immortal quality of the soul is an essential part of *her* nature. But as she is really identified with her soul all the time, her projection of it is mere confusion on her part and does not enter into the mutually projecting bargain of relationship.

It is almost as if a woman were so unconscious of herself that she does not notice that she has breasts so she looks for them on the man and is surprised at his annoyed repudiation. When a man makes love he is, of course, by no means always aware that he is looking for his soul though in fact this probably is so, but for a woman physical union with the soul apparently ignored makes her acutely unhappy. We all know this. But her distress may I believe be mainly due to her own lack of awareness that no man can truly meet her body without also encountering her soul because, as she is identified with soul, her body and her soul are indivisible.

I think it is indisputable that women recognize their own soul quality the moment they think about the matter, but this brings us back to the part of my talk to which I have already alluded: they cannot really focus upon such a thing to the point of being able to see it and realize its meaning without prior development of their masculine side, so that the Logos development of a woman is the essential first step towards her becoming really conscious of her own soul images.

For a woman to be unconsciously identified with her soul may be good enough to enable a man to find his, and for the woman to feel united to her man, but it is a far cry from consciously knowing her own soul quality. For then she looks to the man as the keeper of her soul which only makes him impatiently declare that she is reading more into the relationship than exists (how often we hear that) while she feels sad and belittled. I suggest, however, that the moment a woman recognizes that she does not need to look for her immortal essence in a man, for it is imbedded in and permeates her very body, this mutual exasperation disappears. She may even laugh at herself for having imagined the man was leaving the soul out (just sex as she calls it), while at the same time she frees him from a projection he cannot carry.

In short, whereas man has to find his image of the soul and hold her to him to be complete, it seems that woman has to win by hard work and the prior co-operation of her animus the knowledge that she and her soul are one. May I, before going on, give you another dream showing this father relationship of the animus to the soul: *Here a number of rosy-cheeked children of both sexes joined an obvious animus figure and hailed him as father.* (He had indeed brought these inner figures into being.) *But then running across a field to join him too and calling: 'Father,' the dreamer saw a fey little girl aged seven with a daisy chain on her head who had got left behind.*

This dreamer was a woman of fifty-eight who had had many years of analysis and experience of unconscious imagery, but this fey, ethereal little girl was a very late comer. That she was crowned with the loveliest and earthiest and most child-like of starry flowers seemed a fitting meeting of opposites to depict an image of the soul with its inevitable affinity with the Self.

The meeting of opposites is beautifully portrayed in the paint-ing of a woman of about forty-five. To her own surprise she painted a large winged vase in a luminous cavity beneath the earth. The vase is a typical feminine symbol but this one had no base on which to stand. Its base was a point so it was actually held upright by great spiritual wings. Moreover the luminosity of the spirit is found in the darkness of the earth itself. This woman knew in the dream that this vase was an image of the soul.

Another woman about fifty or so dreamt: *She was travelling on a difficult journey on foot. The path was precipitous and stony and*

*a strong wind was blowing. Sheltered within her two cupped*
*hands was a white moth. To guard the moth from harm was her*
*passionate concern. She was beset with anxiety lest she might trip*
*and bruise its wings or let it fall and be blown away by the wind.*

The dreamer was in Zürich at the time and Toni Wolff un-
hesitatingly declared that the moth represented the woman's soul.
The dreamer had always thought of the moth as she.

Here it seems that the dreamer is warned of the dangers that
beset a woman's soul throughout life and perhaps especially in
analysis. It can be harmed by any false step and actually lost if not
protected from the strong wind of the masculine spirit.

I recall a poem by Edith Sitwell entitled 'The Youth with the
Red-Gold Hair':

> Fear only the red-gold sun with the fleece of a fox
> Who will steal the fluttering bird you hide in your breast.

Are not these lines also a warning that a too bright sun of consciousness is a thief who comes to steal away our treasures, not in
the night but in the day? It is the peril of over-intelectualization to
the soul of man or woman alike — the desperate peril with which
Western man is faced. I often wonder if the dreams of burglars or
frightening men in the basement which are so common to women
may not express woman's fear of the rape of her soul every bit as
much as the fear of the rape of her body.

I think a white moth must be an archetypal image of the soul.
Carla Lanyon has written a poem entitled 'The White Moth'. She
describes a thundery night with windows flung wide to a hot
garden and one lamp burning:

> We talked, a group of friends, young men and women
> Who turned the world with talk to put it right,
> And all the heavens too, because the burden
> Of our argument obliterated God.

Then suddenly she tells how a white moth flew in and settled
above her head, and here is her final verse:

> I saw its furred face, the exact design
> Of three black circles set in a triangle,
> The pure eurythmy of all curve and line;
> A white moth, antennae just a tingle,

Poised like a spirit, consummate, divine.
And I forgot our heady talk and wrangle,
Forgot we had obliterated God.

This I believe is what the poet is never allowed to forget, the existence of the immortal soul.

One woman of about fifty-five dreamt: *She was on a journey alone in some sort of vehicle, travelling across a highish plateau from which she had extensive views. At one point she passed a church on her right hand which she felt she had seen before and which filled her with a warm glow of recognition and delight. It was very old, built of yellow stone. A low squat building with no windows.*

*In the distance she saw another church with two very phallic-looking towers which she knew in the dream to be Manchester. It was unfamiliar and far away but she felt that she must visit it sometime. However before doing so she came to another church where she alighted from her vehicle. There were a number of people outside the big open door of the church all talking to one another. These people she knew in the dream were Jungians and she wondered why they talked so much and why they stayed outside the church instead of going in. It was perhaps because they preferred to stay in the sunshine and open air. These people were all very friendly but she decided not to stay with them and continued her journey. She walked through an arched doorway into the hillside and proceeded along many winding corridors and down staircases (always down never up) until she arrived in the large entrance hall of what was obviously a great mansion. It had a big door to the outside which must of course have been on a much lower level than the three churches she had seen earlier, as she had been coming down all the time.*

*She did not apparently attempt to go out or even look out of the great door for she found herself sitting up in bed in a small waiting room adjoining it. There were two other figures in the room, dark and shadowy. As she sat and wondered who they might be, she glanced through the open door of the waiting room into the entrance hall and there she saw to her astonishment a woman with loose dark springy hair clothed in filmy blue edging her way down the stairs along the blue wall which was exactly the same colour as her dress. She crept as though she were trying to escape detection. Having arrived opposite the door of the waiting room this blue-*

*clad figure looked around carefully to make sure no one was look-*
*ing, then dashed across the hall into the waiting room itself and*
*stood beside the two dark shadowy figures at the foot of the*
*dreamer's bed, who then awoke.*

She did a lot of work on this dream by active imagination and
later she discussed it at length with Mrs. Jung. The old, low,
squat, windowless church with which she had felt so akin seemed
to grow out of the earth and to represent perhaps the spirituality
of the earth itself. The dreamer's own feminine earthiness recognized this church as something to which she belonged. The two-
towered church in the distance clearly represented the spirituality
of Man, for Manchester means the City of Man. This was something about which she knew almost nothing. She had not yet
visited this church. She only saw it in the distance.

The fact that the Jungians stayed outside the next church talking in the sunshine of consciousness expressed no doubt her own
feeling at that time that psychology was not providing her with the
spiritual answer she was seeking. So she did not stay with them but
penetrated the hillside, once more the feminine earth, descending
lower and lower until she found herself in the waiting room within
the great entrance hall of the large mansion.

Active imagination produced the wholly unexpected realization
that the woman in blue, who was so shy of being seen, was a soul
image, and that the two dark shadowy figures whom she joined in
the waiting room were the Emissaries of Death. They appeared as
two, as frequently happens in dreams when something is only
emerging into consciousness and is still too vague for any appre-
hension of distinct qualities.

She has learned since that the Emissaries of Death and the soul
are never far apart, for the soul being man's immortal essence is at
home with death and never ceases to await death's consummation.
One could also say that in the dream the two dark shadowy Emissaries of Death are the dark, menacing, destructive aspects of the
soul of which the woman in blue is the light aspect, so, as opposites, they are invariably found together.

That the soul can be dark, negative and destructive may seem a
strange idea but it is impossible to imagine that the immortal soul
has human attributes such as kindness, courage or forgiveness.
Those are qualities acquired through being mortal and human.
The soul is not human but our immortal essence and I can imagine that anyone who was completely identified with their

M

immortal essence might be an insufferable person to live with and destructive in the extreme to the more vulnerable people around them.

In later years the blue-clad woman has appeared again and again and very often accompanied by another figure who is clearly the Self. If this dreamer consciously attempts to conjure up either the blue woman or her image of the Self the other also appears. It was Mrs. Jung who drew the dreamer's attention to the importance of the waiting room. They had often talked together of waiting as an essential positive quality of the feminine. The feminine in every woman is always waiting. She may not know it if she has another more masculine side which is busy with active achievement but I believe that every woman if she looks deep enough will find that the essential core of her is waiting.

As a tiny girl she waits to be grown-up, filling the time with all sorts of occupations and study, which to the essential growing point are quite irrelevant. As time passes most women quite consciously wait for a coming lover or husband no matter how vociferously they declare the contrary. No woman as woman can plan her future. She can plan a career, but as woman she can only wait for the future to unfold itself. Her lover emerges from the mists of time and in his wake so also does the place where she will dwell. Whether it is near her birthplace or on a distant shore will be determined for her by the love to which she has been elected. It could not be foretold or planned. So she needs must wait and the more conscious women know for what they wait.

A woman is always waiting — she may or may not conceive — she can only wait and see. Nine long months she waits, not knowing whether her child will be son or daughter, dark or fair, morose or gay, brilliant or a dunce. This is equally true in realms of the spirit or the intellect in both men and women. Intellectual achievement when it is not merely mechanical always has to wait for inspiration. It is the feminine which waits whether it is in man or woman and it is the masculine which moulds and formulates in either sex.

Waiting is I believe as essential a part of feminine psychology today as it was for Penelope. The picture of Penelope working at her loom every day as she listened to the wooing entreaties of her many suitors, and undoing her weaving at nightfall so that she could await the return of Ulysses, is I believe the picture of any woman who listens to the seductive voices of collective opinion

and plans her life accordingly yet in the solitude of her own heart
unravels her false weaving every night knowing that it is not planning for the future, but waiting which will bring her future to
her.

A woman once talked to Dr. Jung about a number of things
and ended by asking him, 'What do I do with all this?' 'Just wait,'
he answered, 'and whatever you have to do will come to you.' In a
few years it did so. Feminine spirituality I have likened elsewhere
to the sacred oil which the wise virgins kept always ready in their
lamps waiting, waiting for the coming of the bridegroom.

This is very near the final waiting of the soul for the coming of
death, a constant unceasing waiting throughout every moment of
the span of life, for the soul belongs to death as much as it belongs
to life. I am of course no longer speaking of the soul image but of
the soul itself. It is the rest of our personality which fears to die.
Our animal instinct clings to life, our minds dread the unknown,
and our hearts with good reason tremble lest we may be cut off
before we have carried out the tasks which have been set us, tasks
at which sometimes we can only guess.

It is certainly those who have lived fully who seem least afraid
to die. Perhaps they have left fewer tasks undone. But it is the
feminine soul in man or woman which waits ceaselessly without
fear and without impatience for the coming of death, the last
lover, who will lead to a new unfolding. I am aware that I am
going beyond the boundaries of the provable. I am not out to
prove anything. I am merely offering you the fruits of my own
minute experience, in no attempt to be scientific. If they do not
ring a bell or touch a chord of sympathetic knowing from my
readers it matters not at all.

The idea that the soul has to be humanized seems to be borne
out in the active imagination of a young professional woman
named Jane who had come to analysis because she felt dry and
stale. The moment her natural capacity to fantasize reasserted
itself, she recovered her poise, disentangled herself from the sterile
relationships in which she was caught and fell in love with the
man she married a little later.

In the particular fantasy I am referring to: *She re-entered a
dark room in a large moated country house of which she had
dreamt. There was cold moonlight outside and some men,* (presumably animus figures) *were looking for her. There was no light
in the room other than a large fire, beside which sat a very old*

*woman and a fair-haired little girl. The old woman said to Jane,
'Don't bother about the men who are looking for you. You are
quite safe here within the moat. They can't see anyway even
though there is moonlight. Presently they will fall into the moat
and take their darkness with them. Now you come and play
draughts with me. You take the white and I will be black.' They
sat down and played draughts but the old woman contrived that
Jane should win, seemingly playing the white draughts as well as
her own, though it was Jane's hands which moved them.*

*While the game was in progress Jane noticed that the child
seated by the fire was getting bigger. Her hair was long and looked
wet as though she had come out of the sea. Suddenly three silver
fish leapt out of her mouth into the fire where they swam around
and turned a rosy gold colour, whereupon the girl reached out,
lifted them from the fire and swallowed them again. One could see
them swimming down her throat turning her hitherto white neck
a rosy colour.*

*'Don't bother about her,' said the old lady, 'she is growing up
and has to warm bits of herself outside. They'll stay warm once
they are inside her again.' As she spoke the girl got up and moved
round the room, the three fish inside her producing an odd light
which enabled Jane to see that the walls were covered with beautiful and ancient pictures, tapestries and metal engravings. The girl
moved out into the garden and wherever she walked the lawns
and flowers were lit up until the moonlight could no longer be
noticed. She wandered down the garden and dived into the
moat.*

I dare say some of you will be able to throw more light on this
fantasy but the main things which impressed me are the following:

Within the moated country house which is presumably a
symbol of the Self is found not a wise old man but a wise old
woman. The game of draughts between the old woman and Jane
seems to express an excellent relationship between the Self and
the ego for the Self contrives that though the ego shall win it is in
obedience to the Self. We must have an ego and at this particular
time in Jane's life it was important that she should free herself
from the animus world in which she had been caught (expressed
by the men who were looking for her) and make her own judgments and decisions. It is this which the wise old woman
ensures.

At the same time Jane finds her own soul image seated close beside the old woman and visibly growing.

The three silver fish puzzled me for a long time but I think they must stand for the innate spiritual quality of the soul which only when it has been transformed in the fire of feeling and passion becomes warm and golden so that it glows from within. The cold, impersonal feminine moonlight disappeared when the fish had been warmed in the fire of passion.

Perhaps when the girl dived into the moat she will have illumined the darkness of the animi who had fallen in and they will all emerge together on better terms, but that is only my guess.

The transformation of the fish and the growing of the child both seem to suggest that the innate soul quality needs to be humanized and grow up, perhaps even be made conscious before it can become the golden light that visibly glows, but I think it is important to emphasize that the silver fish came in the first place from *within* the feminine soul figure and are not something imbibed from without.

May I conclude with a dream of my own: *I was walking arm in arm with Barbara Hannah.* (Miss Hannah is for me the person of all the Jungians who has penetrated most deeply into feminine psychology, as in her memorable and far-reaching lecture on 'Women's Plots' and the light she has thrown on women's creativity in her studies of the Brontë sisters.)[5] *I was walking with her on the hillside when we came to a stairway leading down into the bowels of the earth. We proceeded down this stair together until we reached a long gallery with beds in it looking rather like a hospital ward. In the floor we found a trap-door which we lifted disclosing a still more rugged stone stairway leading yet further down. I descended this stair alone until it ended in a rope ladder hovering above a sea in which strange primitive reptilian beasts were swimming, and among them one woman with long flowing hair in evident great distress. I did not dare swim out to her unaided. But two men came to my rescue, one my former analyst with whom I was still in touch, another a man of actual importance in my life. These fastened two ropes around my waist and each held one, so that I could be held safe and pulled back again. With this assurance I swam out to the woman and the men pulled both of us to safety.*

[5] B. Hannah, *Striving Towards Wholeness*, C. G. Jung Foundation, New York, 1971.

*The woman was either too exhausted or too bewildered to walk, but we three dragged her up to the hospital ward and were about to put her to bed when an authoritative voice rang out: 'It is no use leaving her there,' it said, 'she must be taken up into the sunlight.'*
*With the help of other people who were about we got her up the last lap of stairway. The sun was shining brilliantly and we laid her on the grass.*

If it had not been for this dream I doubt if I should be giving this talk today for it put me on the alert. To me the dream is saying that the feminine soul image of a woman is still in great distress because it has remained in the unconscious and it desperately needs to be brought into consciousness.

The hospital ward is, I suggest, the level of the unconscious where healing takes place in analysis. It is the region of deliberate organized healing. It is not enough to bring this distressed figure into the sphere of analysis. She needs to be brought right up into the consciousness of every day.

The role of the two men in the dream is of paramount importance. Taken as inner animus figures they represent the power to focus, make conscious and give meaning to what I saw. But they are also actual men with whom I had a close relationship. They stand for reality and it was, I think, only because I had this double hold on reality, both analytical and personal, that I could risk swimming quite so far out of my depth.

This paper, inadequate as it must inevitably be, is my first attempt to get this distressed feminine figure out into the light of day where she can be acknowledged and accepted. I cannot possibly succeed alone.

My paper, more than anything else, is an appeal to all of those of you who feel the task worthwhile, to help lift this figure, which I believe to be the image of the feminine soul of woman, right up into the sunshine and lag her on the green, growing grass of conscious reality.

*Index*

# Index